MARIJUANA

Praise for *Marijuana: The Unbiased Truth about the World's Most Popular Weed*

"It's delightful to see such a thorough, accessible review of such a diverse literature, even from an accomplished author who doesn't view the research the way that I do. It reminds us that reasonable people can differ and still stay reasonable. Check out this text for the latest on this controversial topic."

MITCH EARLEYWINE, PHD, Professor and Director of Clinical Training, University at Albany, SUNY, Author of *Understanding Marijuana* (Oxford University Press), Chair of the Executive Board of NORML (National Organization for the Reform of Marijuana Laws)

"The risks of marijuana use are widely debated and disagreed about—from questions of addiction and withdrawal, to effectiveness in treating various medical problems, to degrees of harmfulness and lasting deleterious changes. . . . What has been missing is a *balanced approach* to all of these issues—an approach present in this volume by Dr. Kevin P. Hill. The book covers a wide range of topics in a thoughtful and comprehensive manner. Both pro- and anti-marijuana individuals will find material that agrees with their positions—and challenges them. . . . It can be usefully read and consulted by health professionals, policy makers, law enforcement, parents, teachers, and students."

HERBERT D. KLEBER, MD, Director, Division on Substance Abuse, New York State Psychiatric Institute

"Bravo to Dr. Hill for taking on the task of explaining in detail the scientific and clinical information related to the controversial aspects of marijuana use, addiction, and legalization. He brings his personal, professional, and scientific knowledge to the table in an effort to provide readers with much more than a cursory overview of the issues. Novice readers will come away with broad knowledge of the field, and those who have already formed opinions will be forced to rethink their positions."

ALAN J. BUDNEY, PHD, professor of psychiatry at the Geisel School of Medicine, Dartmouth

MARIJUANA

THE UNBIASED TRUTH ABOUT
THE WORLD'S MOST POPULAR WEED

KEVIN P. HILL, MD, MHS

Hazelden Publishing

Hazelden Publishing
Center City, Minnesota 55012
hazelden.org/bookstore

ISBN: 978-1-61649-559-6

Library of Congress Cataloging-in-Publication Data
is on file with the Library of Congress.

Editor's notes

The names, details, and circumstances may have been changed to protect the privacy of those mentioned in this publication.

This publication is not intended as a substitute for the advice of health care professionals.

Alcoholics Anonymous, AA, and the Big Book are registered trademarks of Alcoholics Anonymous World Services, Inc.

19 18 17 16 15   1 2 3 4 5 6

Developmental editor: Sid Farrar
Production editor: Heather Silsbee
Cover design by Kathi Dunn, Dunn + Associates
Interior design and typesetting by Percolator

*To my wife, Debbie, and
my daughters, Hannah and Sophie*

CONTENTS

SECTION IV: TREATMENT

LIST OF FIGURES

PREFACE

Marijuana has been in the news constantly as American states and countries around the world have been asked to make important decisions about medical marijuana and the legalization of marijuana for recreational use. These decisions have led to heated debates about the benefits and risks of marijuana use. People often have strong opinions about marijuana and, at times, these opinions obscure the scientific realities of the drug. This book is designed to help separate fact from opinion in the hopes that a better understanding of marijuana will allow people to make educated choices about marijuana use, medical marijuana, and legalization. The book also aims to provide a framework for recognizing marijuana addiction and tips for what you can do to help.

My goal is to be as objective as possible when covering the complex questions surrounding this drug. However, I'm sure that my personal experiences will still come through in my writing. Addiction is a part of all my days. I am an addiction psychiatrist at McLean Hospital and assistant professor of psychiatry at Harvard Medical School. My work focuses on three areas: clinical work, clinical research, and education. Every day of the week I see patients in several clinical arenas:

- I am the director of the Substance Abuse Consultation Service and see patients regularly in that role.

- I teach and supervise psychiatry resident physicians, where we see patients with addiction problems in various specialty units of the hospital.

- I also see patients while leading three clinical trials at McLean that aim to develop effective treatments for addiction; I see the rest of my patients as a part of my small private practice.

Patients with addictions are referred to me from a variety of sources, including colleagues from all over and organizations that I consult with, such as the NFL (National Football League) and the FAA (Federal Aviation Administration). I help my patients battle their addictions so that they can function in the other important areas of their lives, such as work, school, and relationships.

But it is not only my experience as an MD that has helped me understand just how damaging alcohol and other drugs can be. My strong family history of addiction forced me think about this disease and its ramifications at a young age. My grandfather lived four houses down the block from us in Rochester, New York, and his drinking progressed after the death of my grandmother. My brothers and I loved and respected my grandfather, and we liked to go to his house each day to see what he was up to. There were days when my mother did not let us go there—I remember wondering why we couldn't go, and I then recall connecting this to the unusual number of large empty Chablis bottles that lined his curb every Wednesday for the next day's garbage collection.

Seeing a bright, accomplished person drinking every day to the detriment of other areas of his life had a profound impact on me, one that stuck with me as I became involved in addiction research as an undergraduate at Skidmore College. I needed to understand how addiction happened and how to control it. I made the challenge of finding treatments for addiction my life's work and I have been at it ever since, working with thousands of patients.

While there has been a lot of progress in understanding the causes, progression, and treatment of addiction, especially over the past twenty years, I am constantly reminded how far we still have to go. My patients remind me of this, but an incident with a family member is even more compelling for me personally. I live with the memory of sitting helplessly at my desk in my Belmont, Massachusetts, office upon learning that my uncle, who suffered from alcoholism and depression, committed suicide by jumping off a thirteen-story building. Although I had been in touch with those treating my uncle, and although I know that both alcoholism and depression are very difficult diseases to treat, I still feel as if I let my uncle and my family down. This feeling has motivated me to push even harder in my work to treat addiction.

While my interest in addiction has been long-standing, I have focused on marijuana for the past four years. As an attending psychiatrist in the McLean Hospital addictions program, I saw patient after patient seeking treatment for opioid addiction and alcohol addiction. When I sat with these patients and took a careful, detailed history, however, I found that more than half of them described a lengthy time in their lives when they were smoking marijuana daily. I wondered what would happen if, during that time when they smoked every day, they were able to get the right kind of help to stop. How would this affect their lives? Would they be as likely to end up in treatment for opioid or alcohol addiction down the road?

Ever since, I have been trying to find a way to effectively intervene on people's daily marijuana use and minimize the risk of addiction.

The third area of my professional focus, education, has been especially important in the past two years, as marijuana policy issues have claimed public interest. I have extended my teaching about marijuana and marijuana addiction from other doctors and health care professionals to the general public. That is what this book is about.

ACKNOWLEDGMENTS

There are many people I must thank for their support of my work. First and foremost, I would like to thank the patients I have worked with over the years: without them this book would not be possible. They have allowed me into their lives, and I have been fortunate to have that privilege. My patients have taught me more about marijuana than any other source. I continue to learn from my patients, and my work is an extension of their generosity.

My family has supported me throughout my career. My wife, Debbie, is a staunch supporter of mine who has made many sacrifices to make it easier for me to do what I need to do. My daughters, Hannah and Sophie, help me stay grounded by reminding me where I am on the family totem pole. My parents, Anne and Larry Hill, have always given me the opportunity to excel; my mother is especially skilled at listening when things are not moving along as well I would like them to be. I thank my older brother, Matt, for his unconditional support from the beginning. My younger brother, Justin, supports me as well, and, as an assistant district attorney in Livingston County, New York, he helped me better understand several legal aspects of marijuana.

My wife's parents, Helen and Howard Siegel, and my wife's sister, Jen Siegel, have also supported my efforts for years.

Professionally, I have had the good fortune to have excellent role models. Along the way, Jean Bidlack, PhD, Ashwin Patkar, MD, Harlan Krumholz, MD, Mehmet Sofuoglu, MD, PhD, and Gary Gottlieb, MD, have all played instrumental roles in my development as a physician scientist. At McLean Hospital currently, my mentors Shelly Greenfield, MD, MPH, Scott Lukas, PhD, and Roger Weiss, MD, have shared their experiences with me while allowing me the freedom to explore my own limits.

I am grateful to the National Institute on Drug Abuse, the Brain and Behavior Research Foundation, the American Lung Association, and the Greater Boston Council on Alcoholism for funding my research, although these organizations did not provide support for this book. The views I express do not imply any endorsement by any of these funding agencies.

I thank John Martin-Joy, MD, a friend and former supervisor of mine, for his steadfast faith in my talent as a writer; he encouraged me to educate as many people as possible through this book and through seminars on marijuana. George Vaillant, MD, and Edward Hallowell, MD, were kind enough to point me in the right direction when I was beginning the book-writing process. Dana Newman, my literary agent, has been exceedingly patient throughout the process. My research assistant, Max Hurley-Welljams-Dorof, has spent many hours of his own time helping me with this book in a variety of ways.

Finally, I'd like to thank my editor, Vince Hyman, for encouraging me during the process and pushing at the right times. Vince's editorial skill and willingness to discuss my hopes for the book resulted in a final draft that is much, much stronger than the original.

INTRODUCTION

The issues surrounding marijuana use are complicated, to say the least. Consider the case of Scott, a nineteen-year-old sophomore from a prestigious local university who came to see me about an open court case in which he was involved.

Scott

Scott had been arrested in a local town with about three ounces of marijuana and charged with possession with intent to distribute in a school zone. His case had been continued, or postponed, the same day as our meeting. It was clear that he was sitting in my office that day because he wanted to solve his legal problem and not his marijuana problem.

Scott had a history of anxiety for which he was recently started on the medication fluoxetine (Prozac), and he had smoked marijuana daily for most of the past four years. After getting charged with possession and intent to distribute, he smoked a few more times "as a send-off," but he said that he had not smoked in twenty-five days and was not going to smoke again "until these charges get cleared up." He said that he felt marijuana actually helped his anxiety and that, before these charges, he had not experienced any problems related to his use. He proudly pointed out that he was carrying a 3.3 GPA despite his daily smoking. He said he sold marijuana so "I could smoke when I wanted and I could smoke up my friends too." While he was distressed by the daily anxiety he experienced and worried that it was only getting worse, he was not willing to consider the possibility that daily marijuana use might be contributing to his anxiety. Scott agreed to see a therapist and to undergo random drug testing. He was on probation for a year before all of his charges were cleared.

Scott's case raises many issues that we will address in this book. Was Scott medicating his anxiety with a relatively harmless drug, while enjoying it recreationally like thousands of other people? Or, was he addicted to marijuana and was the drug making his anxiety worse instead of helping it? How much did his daily marijuana use affect his school performance? At what point should people seek professional help for their marijuana use, and how do they know if they are addicted and in need of treatment? The legal questions raised by Scott's case are also considerable. Should marijuana be legal and, if so, how should it be sold? If illegal, what should be the penalties for selling marijuana? And does our legal system treat marijuana use and sale by people of different ethnic groups inconsistently?

This book is divided into four sections: the Problem, the Three Myths, Policy, and Treatment.

Section 1, the Problem, sets the tone for the rest of the book by describing the context in which marijuana has become such a hot topic and also explaining the complexities of the statistics of marijuana use. In chapter 1, "Why Is Marijuana So Misunderstood?," I explain why there is a gap between the science of marijuana and the public perception of it. It is important to understand the physical nature of the drug and its history in order to appreciate its popularity—especially in light of recent headlines—as state legislatures debate about the merits of medical marijuana and legalization of the drug.

Marijuana has received its fair share of negative publicity over the years, with the tide of public sentiment turning recently. Many of today's celebrities seem to go out of their way to publicize their use of the drug. Unfortunately, media coverage tends to promote common misperceptions about marijuana, which may be contributing to the 2012 Monitoring the Future data showing that, unlike usage trends for other drugs, use of marijuana among young people is on the rise and, perhaps even more alarming, perception of risk is on the decline. In this first chapter, we explore this gap in knowledge and review the major reasons why people have difficulty understanding the data on marijuana.

In chapter 2, "A Small Fraction of a Large Number Can Be a Very Large Number," I tackle the confusing statistics surrounding marijuana use. More people use marijuana than any other illicit drug, and more people meet criteria for addiction to marijuana than to any other illicit drug. Yet, we hear more about the opioid epidemic, with misuse of prescription opioids like Vicodin and OxyContin increasing and large numbers of opioid users eventually beginning to inject heroin, a cheaper alternative to prescription opioids. While the concern about the opioid problem is both warranted and understandable, it is puzzling that we do not hear more about the potential dangers of marijuana, especially considering the large numbers of Americans affected by it. The silence may be due in part to the insidious, or slow-to-develop, nature of the effects of marijuana addiction. When treating those with addictions, we do not see people come into treatment for marijuana addiction as a result of catastrophic events. It is true that no one overdoses on marijuana like they might on opioids, for example.

In section 2, the Three Myths, I discuss the three major myths that contribute to the gap between the science of marijuana and the public's perception of the drug. In chapter 3, "Myth #1: Marijuana Is Not Harmful," I confront the alarming fact that many Americans believe marijuana to be a harmless drug. Upon finding out the focus of my work, other doctors have even told me that they thought marijuana was not addictive in

the same way as heroin, cocaine, and other drugs they routinely deal with. If you stop the next ten people you see and
ask them about marijuana withdrawal, you will be met with at
least nine blank stares. As a society, we do not consider marijuana to be a potentially dangerous drug like heroin, cocaine,
methamphetamine—or alcohol, which is responsible for more
illnesses and deaths than all other drugs combined, with the
exception of nicotine. Perhaps this is because marijuana occurs
naturally or because many of us have had experiences with
marijuana without major consequences. In this critical chapter,
I translate the scientific literature that spells out the dangers of
marijuana use. I review recent studies, including brain-imaging
studies that show regular marijuana use negatively impacts cognitive function. These studies underscore the significant risk of
regular marijuana use on the developing brains of adolescents.
Rigorous research also documents the association between
marijuana use and both anxiety and depression. While many
smoke marijuana to relieve anxiety, I describe how marijuana
actually worsens anxiety. Finally, I address the chilling research
that shows that, for those who are at risk of psychosis, marijuana use increases the likelihood of developing psychosis and
corresponding illnesses such as schizophrenia.

In chapter 4, "Myth #2: Marijuana Use Cannot Lead to Addiction," I discuss how the science illustrates that marijuana—
considered a "soft drug" by many—is more similar to "hard
drugs" like heroin and cocaine than it is different. I will describe
marijuana's effects upon brain chemistry, including how use
of marijuana leads to surges of dopamine—a neurotransmitter that helps control the brain's pleasure and reward center.
Other drugs and addictive behaviors such as overeating, sex,
and gambling cause the same type of surges. These surges help
to explain why some people smoke marijuana every day despite
obvious harm to other areas of their lives. In this chapter, we

will hear directly from patients as they talk about why they smoke every day and how hard it has been for them to stop. We also address the genetic predisposition to marijuana addiction. Why are some people more likely than others to become addicted to marijuana? Why do some people with a genetic predisposition for marijuana addiction actually end up addicted while others with similar genes do not become addicted?

Chapter 5, "Myth #3: Stopping Use of Marijuana Does Not Cause Withdrawal," introduces the concept of withdrawal from addictive substances and shows how such withdrawal does occur when people who use marijuana regularly try to stop using abruptly. Very few people are aware that stopping use of marijuana can cause withdrawal. We will look at a case example to see how withdrawal works. From a patient's point of view, we will hear in vivid detail about the anxiety, irritability, and insomnia associated with marijuana withdrawal. We will also review the scientific studies that lucidly demonstrate a marijuana withdrawal syndrome as distinct as that associated with nicotine withdrawal. The miserable feelings withdrawal causes often lead to relapse. When many of my patients learn about marijuana withdrawal they are relieved, as it validates the difficulties they've experienced in stopping use of marijuana.

In section 3, Policy, we shift gears into a discussion of the hot-button marijuana policy issues that have been all over the news in the past few years. We start with chapter 6, "Decriminalization and Legalization of Recreational Marijuana," which describes both the initial decriminalization laws of recreational marijuana and the question that states around the country are now facing: should marijuana be legalized? Although marijuana remains an illegal drug according to the U.S. government, several states have decriminalized recreational marijuana. As of the time of this writing, four states, Washington, Colorado, Alaska, and Oregon, as well as the District of Columbia, have voted to legalize recreational marijuana. And I'm sure this is only the beginning of a growing trend. Decriminalization of marijuana usually means that possession of an amount of marijuana associated with "personal use" only carries the threat of a civil penalty. In Massachusetts, for example, possession of less than one ounce of marijuana—enough to roll about fifty-six joints—results in only a civil penalty, most likely a fine. The result of a statute many find to be toothless is that law enforcement personnel often do not bother enforcing marijuana-related offenses. Legalization has also been pushed forward by marijuana advocates; in November 2012, Washington and Colorado voted to treat marijuana like alcohol, restricting legal possession to residents age twenty-one and older. This is a complex issue without easy answers, so we must carefully consider both sides of the legalization debate.

In chapter 7, "Medical Marijuana: The Science and Practical Implications," we review how twenty-three states and the District of Columbia have passed laws to implement medical marijuana programs. Thus, it is important to understand the pros and cons of medical marijuana from a theoretical standpoint. There are patients with terminal cancer and other terrible diseases who feel that marijuana provides relief that they cannot find with any other medications, including dronabinol (oral delta-9-tetrahydrocannabinol, THC, the active ingredient responsible for the euphoric effects of marijuana), and this may be due in part to the presence of cannabidiol, one of the active ingredients in the marijuana plant. There are likely reasons for the groundswell of public support for medical marijuana, and we talk about those reasons in chapter 7. I also review the medical marijuana laws that have been passed around the country. Clinicians are eager to know how to respond when approached by patients about medical marijuana, and I offer practical advice on what to do in these situations.

In section 4: Treatment, I cover all aspects of treatment, from diagnosis to the types of treatments available. Chapter 8, "Never Worry Alone: Finding Help for Someone Who May Have a Problem," starts with the fact that most people with addiction problems do not seek treatment, and those with marijuana addiction are no different. As we discuss in section 2, many Americans do not think of marijuana addiction as something that would require treatment. Furthermore, if it is decided that someone may need treatment, most people do not know what treatment actually entails. This is no one's fault; treatment for marijuana addiction is complex. So, the message of this chapter is simple: If you or someone you care about may be addicted to marijuana, never worry alone. Reach out to treatment facilities, your primary care doctor, or your child's school nurse. They can help you figure out what type of evaluation and treatment is necessary.

Unfortunately, the way that television programs depict the treatment of substance use disorders is rarely realistic. Insurance-based treatment usually means an evaluation with an addictions clinician: a psychiatrist, psychologist, or licensed clinical social worker. Patients for whom marijuana use is causing significant problems usually end up in outpatient care, either with an individual therapist or in a structured treatment program like an intensive outpatient program. In this chapter, we also describe other elements of treatment such as family support and self-help groups like Marijuana Anonymous.

In chapter 9, "Behavioral Interventions as Treatment for Marijuana Addiction," I describe behavioral interventions, or "talk therapies," and how they can help people make significant reductions in their smoking. In this section we review the recent scientific literature on behavioral interventions for marijuana addiction. Motivational interviewing is a strategy that is helpful for engaging prospective patients in treatment when they are ambivalent or unsure about whether they need or want treatment. Successful motivational interviewing involves acknowledging that there are aspects of marijuana use that patients enjoy while also attempting to help patients realize and express why it may be wise for them to either reduce their use of marijuana or stop altogether. The data suggests that the type of talk therapy a clinician chooses at this juncture is not as important as the duration of treatment and the skill level of the therapist. Cognitive behavioral therapy (CBT) is another "talk" therapy where the therapist and patient explore the connection between thoughts, feelings, and behaviors in specific instances in which the patient typically uses marijuana.

Chapter 10, "Using Medications to Treat Marijuana Addiction," covers the medication options that may help people stop smoking marijuana and remain abstinent. Despite the alarming numbers of Americans addicted to marijuana and the trends that suggest those numbers are increasing, there are no FDA-approved medications for treating marijuana addiction. Ultimately, we expect that a combination of a behavioral intervention and a medication will be the treatment of choice for marijuana addiction. Research on other mental illnesses, such as depression, suggests that patients would fare better if they receive a combination of behavioral therapy and medication than they would with treatment of either one alone.

In chapter 11, "The Effect of Marijuana Addiction on Loved Ones," we address how families are affected when people are addicted to marijuana. Even when the person with a problem agrees to seek treatment and engages in it, the entire process can be draining for the family. We begin by describing an approach that family members can take before treatment is initiated to make it more likely that their family member enters a treatment program and more likely that the family itself not only survives the process but emerges healthier. We discuss various resources available to families with members who are addicted and how to access these resources. Just as the family member with an addiction will have to learn how to manage the addiction for the rest of his or her life, the family also must come to grips with the notion that a loved one has a lifelong medical problem that will likely affect the family in many ways.

We conclude by attempting to answer the question "Where Do We Go from Here?" Marijuana is an issue that is not going away. As a nation, we must work to better understand this drug in order to craft sensible policies on its use. Similarly, there is a long road ahead in the battle to help those with a marijuana addiction stay off the drug or, at the very least, make significant reductions in their use. As noted earlier, the data is concerning—among our young people, use of marijuana is on the rise and the perception of risk is declining. However, the data showing the potential harms of marijuana is clear and strong. Although most people who use marijuana do not develop problems with addiction, for those who do, it is very serious. We are fighting an uphill battle in two ways:

1. Most people are not aware of how dangerous marijuana can be.

2. There is no consensus on the most effective treatment for marijuana addiction.

Ultimately, I aim to present the facts about marijuana in an evidence-based, balanced fashion. People need to know the facts if they are to make educated choices about using marijuana or on how they will vote on the issues of medical marijuana and legalization of marijuana for recreational use. I also want to let those who may want treatment know that there are resources available to help them. If your views on marijuana are set— either pro or con—this book will succeed to the degree that it shakes up those views a bit. If you think marijuana provides only a pleasant high with minimal risks, you will learn that marijuana addiction is real, and marijuana use by adolescents is very damaging to the physical development of their brain. If you think marijuana is an evil drug that leads people down the path of moral degradation, you will find that there are potential medical benefits to be drawn from the chemicals contained in the cannabis plant and that many beliefs about marijuana are not grounded in fact. As you will see, the social, medical, and health issues surrounding marijuana are complex. As with other matters of risk and benefit, there are no easy answers. Let's begin by examining the history of our misunderstanding about this herb and drug.

SECTION I

THE PROBLEM

1

Why Is Marijuana So Misunderstood?

Most of us have little knowledge of marijuana's long and fascinating history. Our society is famous for its short memory. That's too bad, because the long view on marijuana matters. If you observe how it has been viewed over millennia—from sacred or mystical herb, to ancient healing drug, to a symbol of peace, love, and anti-authoritarian freedom—you gain a new respect for the drug. And you can begin to separate fact from trendy public opinion. Armed with data, you can begin to think carefully about just how we should be dealing with the real risks and benefits of this extraordinary plant.

From Mystic Herb to Adolescent Joyride

Over the past one hundred years, public opinion on marijuana in the United States has been on a roller-coaster ride. Worldwide, however, marijuana has been used for medical, sacred, and recreational purposes for at least 5,000 years.[1] Marijuana goes by many different names, including pot, weed, bud, grass, reefer, herb, Mary Jane, and MJ. The drug consists of dried plant products—leaves, stems, seeds, and flowers—of the cannabis, or hemp, plant. The most common varieties are *Cannabis sativa* and *Cannabis indica*. Marijuana is thought to have originated in Central Asia and is found all over the world today.

Marijuana has been used medicinally around the globe for thousands of years. The Chinese emperor Fu Hsi referred to marijuana as a popular medicine in 2900 BC, and it was included in the Chinese Pharmacopeia, the *Rh-Ya*, in 1500 BC. By AD 100, the Chinese had identified more than 100 medical uses for marijuana, including as a treatment for gout and malaria. Marijuana was a part of a "holy anointing oil" referenced in the original Hebrew version of the book of Exodus. The ancient Egyptians prescribed marijuana as a medical treatment for such problems as glaucoma and inflammation. In India around 1000 BC (3,000 years ago), bhang, a drink that consisted of marijuana and milk, was used as an anesthetic and antiphlegmatic. By 600 BC, the Indians had expanded their belief in marijuana's healing properties to include prolonging life, improving cognitive abilities and judgment, reducing fever, inducing sleep, and curing such maladies as dysentery and leprosy. Persians thought highly of marijuana as well, listing it in 700 BC as the most important of 10,000 medicinal plants, while the Greeks of 200 BC used it as a medical remedy for earaches, swelling, and inflammation.

The Romans found it to be useful as well. In AD 70, a Roman army medical text stated that "kannabis" could treat earaches and suppress sexual desires. Shortly thereafter, the Roman author Pliny the Elder documented that the roots of the marijuana plant could be boiled in water and used to treat arthritis, gout, and pain. In Arabia between AD 800 and 900, marijuana was used to treat a host of medical problems, including migraines, syphilis, and pain. The English noted many medical uses for marijuana, starting with clergyman Robert Burton recommending marijuana as a treatment for depression in his book *The Anatomy of Melancholy*. Other Englishmen touted marijuana, usually as a tincture that was ingested, as a treatment for gout, joint pain, muscle spasms, menstrual cramps, rheumatism, convulsions; to promote uterine contractions in childbirth; and as a sleep aid.

Marijuana has had an interesting history in the United States, with the plant playing many different roles in agriculture, industry, medicine, recreation, and religion. In colonial America, farmers like George Washington were primarily interested in hemp as a fiber, but Washington wondered about the medicinal properties of the plant in his diary of 1765. Even though it eventually became illegal to grow it in most states, you can't get high from cannabis grown for hemp purposes. Hemp contains very little of the cannabinoid delta-9-tetrahydrocannabinol (THC) that produces the feeling of euphoria.

Marijuana had become a part of mainstream Western medicine by 1840, and it was added to the U.S. Pharmacopeia in 1850. By this time, new uses such as appetite stimulation, treatment of opioid withdrawal, and suppression of nausea and vomiting had been identified. From 1900 to 1930 in the United States, marijuana was included as part of several medications. In fact, the American pharmaceutical companies Parke-Davis and Eli Lilly marketed cannabis extracts for use as an analgesic (painkiller), antispasmodic (a drug that suppresses muscle spasms), and a sedative. Grimault & Co. sold marijuana cigarettes as a treatment for asthma. In 1928, the tide shifted against the medical use of marijuana, when the drug was prohibited in the United Kingdom under its "Dangerous Drugs Act." At the same time, Harry Anslinger, the commissioner of the Federal Bureau of Narcotics, led efforts to criminalize marijuana in the United States. Anslinger said that marijuana led to insanity and made it more likely that users would commit criminal acts. As a result, all states had enacted laws regulating marijuana by 1936. Anslinger's influence also led to the Marihuana Tax Act of 1937, which aimed to hamper the sale and use of marijuana by taxing it heavily. More and more, physicians were recommending opioids instead of marijuana. By 1942 marijuana was removed from the U.S. Pharmacopeia, with most physicians viewing marijuana as having no medical value.

At this same time, when all states were enacting laws to regulate marijuana, the most important film in marijuana's history was released. Due in part to the portrayal of the drug in the film *Reefer Madness,* which was released in 1936, people feared marijuana as a drug that could make them lose their minds and cause dangerous and violent behavior. Originally intended as a film to teach young people about the dangers of marijuana, *Reefer Madness* was purchased by a producer who edited the film to create the sensationalistic portrayal of rape, suicide, and psychosis that made the film famous. The movie was a significant step backward from a legitimate discussion of the risks and benefits of marijuana, one that still echoes today as many pro-marijuana advocates rightfully deride the movie as a symbol of marijuana fearmongering. *Reefer Madness* deepened the demonization of a drug that, as we have seen, was thought to have widespread medical benefit according to cultures around the world. The movie set an unfortunate precedent in the fascinating story of marijuana—the tendency for people to present biased, and at times comically absurd, characterizations of it. Keep in mind, marijuana has not changed in one respect for thousands of years—it is a drug that is potentially useful and harmful at the same time. Instead it is society's view of marijuana that has changed, shifting back and forth and back, again and again.

The negative hype around marijuana that was started with *Reefer Madness* has continued for generations. At times this hype has been overshadowed by positive messages about marijuana, akin to where things stand today. The effort to demonize marijuana also began another disturbing trend in the marijuana conversation—the habit of tying marijuana use to the negative stereotypes attached to ethnic groups, subcultures, and counter-cultures. Mexican Americans, African Americans, bohemians, jazz musicians, and, more recently, rap artists have all been associated with marijuana use in a negative fashion. For example, marijuana use was popular in Texas border towns in the early 1900s, and law enforcement in these towns derided the plant as a drug of the Mexicans, whom they saw as immoral. A similar scenario played out at the same time in New Orleans, where African Americans, especially African American jazz musicians, smoked "muggles"—marijuana cigarettes—and marijuana use was tied to crime and addicted youths. These associations were unfortunate and remain so to the extent that they have continued for generations; it makes little sense to malign a group's marijuana use when the data shows that marijuana use is not bounded to any particular race, ethnicity, age, or gender.[2]

Opinions about marijuana shifted to a more positive outlook around 1950. Marijuana was popular with artists and musicians during the "Beat Generation" of the 1950s, and its popularity peaked in the 1960s as college students and hippies experimented with drugs, including marijuana. During this period, many people believed it was nothing more than a harmless high. The 1980s and 1990s saw a shift back toward thinking that marijuana was indeed a problem, that it was a "gateway" to more serious drugs like cocaine and heroin. In the past decade, a shift has occurred to the current state of public opinion, with most thinking that marijuana is not very harmful at all, especially as the movements for medical marijuana and legalization of marijuana have progressed.

Marijuana as Medicine

As already noted, people recognized the powerful properties of the marijuana plant thousands of years ago. Millions of people throughout recorded history have enjoyed the calming euphoria, or high, that it produces. People who use marijuana today continue to use it to relax or to enhance their favorite recreational activities. But they have also rediscovered what has been known by many cultures for centuries, that marijuana has tremendous potential as a treatment for a host of medical problems and illnesses. While a large number of marijuana users say that they use it regularly to manage symptoms of anxiety or difficulty sleeping, a growing number of people attest to marijuana's ability to provide relief for a wide array of medical problems, from AIDS to Crohn's disease.

The research supporting marijuana use for this vast array of problems varies greatly, illustrating the wide gap between the science of marijuana and the public perception of it. For the treatment of nausea and vomiting related to cancer chemotherapy, or appetite stimulation due to wasting illnesses like AIDS, the data supporting the benefits of cannabinoids—the chemical compounds of which marijuana is composed—is very strong. As a result, two cannabinoids, dronabinol and nabilone, have been approved by the U.S. Food and Drug Administration (FDA) for these purposes.[3] At the other extreme, while many people have spoken of the potential of cannabinoids as a treatment for amyotrophic lateral sclerosis (ALS—also known as Lou Gehrig's disease)—and multiple states include ALS on their list of illnesses that can be treated with medical marijuana—there has been only one randomized clinical trial on using a cannabinoid to treat ALS. And the results were not positive. Objective observers—and there are far too few involved in the marijuana debate—understand the legitimate data-driven uses, or medical indications, for cannabinoids and look to the future for additional research to support more appropriate uses. At the same time, though, objective observers should be leery when biased individuals, while perhaps well-meaning, ask to make marijuana available to treat illnesses for which there is little or no data to support the effectiveness of marijuana as a treatment.

Learning to Live in the Gray Area

As we're learning, marijuana and the issues surrounding it are complex, but many involved in the marijuana debate try to make it a simpler issue than it is. Smart, dedicated people whom I respect are entrenched on both sides of this polarizing issue. They want it to be a black-and-white issue, but to be truly objective about the pros and cons of marijuana, one has to be comfortable in a gray area. Both sides of the debate—people who feel that any marijuana use will set you off on the road to ruin and people who trumpet the medical applications of marijuana while downplaying its risks—typically choose not to acknowledge data that does not support their platform. This lack of objectivity, coupled with the powerful emotions that are usually attached to this debate, prevent society from making the progress it should with respect to marijuana policy as well as treatment for marijuana addiction.

Being comfortable in the gray area makes progress in policy, as well as progress in treatment, possible. When those both for and against marijuana battle over issues like medical marijuana, they sometimes tend to emphasize only studies that support their side of the argument without acknowledging that some points from the other side have merit. This sort of "cherry-picking" escalates the emotions surrounding the issue, and compromise rarely results from emotional debates. The same holds true from a clinical perspective. If patients come to see me for help in stopping their marijuana use and the first thing I do is toss them a stack of scientific journal articles while reprimanding them for using and questioning their sanity, it's unlikely those patients will want to work with me. This is why we must attempt to be as balanced as possible, from an evidence-based stance, in order to make progress from either a policy or a clinical perspective.

The massive gap between the science of marijuana and the public perception of its use will make this an uphill battle. If we took fifty people aside on a crowded street and asked them about the risks of marijuana, many would tell us that marijuana is harmless and others would say that it automatically leads to addiction or the use of "harder" drugs. Neither of these perspectives is accurate. As we will explore in chapter 2, most people who use marijuana do not become addicted to it, but some will develop an addiction, and that addiction causes problems that are every bit as serious as those caused by "hard drugs" like cocaine and opioids.

How can we become comfortable with the gray area and make both public policy and personal decisions accordingly? Well, it helps to consider another well-known drug that lives in the gray area: alcohol. The comparison between marijuana and alcohol is a useful one. Alcohol is far and away the most commonly used drug, and, as with marijuana, most people who use alcohol do not become addicted to it. A key difference, however, is that we recognize that alcohol can be dangerous. As a result, our society has taken steps to regulate alcohol use and to limit the risks associated with it. Alcohol is heavily taxed and restrictions are placed on its use with respect to age of users and driving after drinking. While alcohol abuse is rampant in movies and on television, we also see public service announcements, and even advertisements by alcoholic beverage producers, promoting the responsible use of alcohol. Many bartenders today receive training on how to monitor their patrons and take steps to decrease the likelihood that someone gets behind the wheel after consuming too much alcohol. Similarly, in some states those who host gatherings where alcohol is consumed assume legal responsibility for the alcohol consumption of their guests.

And DUI laws in the United States have been getting stricter nationally with the penalties getting harsher state by state.

Granted, there certainly have been problems with messaging around the use of alcohol, but the point is that for all the similarities between alcohol and marijuana, there has been little effort to address issues like responsible use of marijuana in a reasonable way. While marijuana remains an illegal drug according to the U.S. government, the prevalence of state medical marijuana laws and the movements toward legalizing the recreational use of marijuana suggest that we should be much further along in tackling the same issues we have addressed with alcohol. It may be too much to ask to address regulatory and responsible use issues before we have laws on its use, but there is no excuse for not confronting these issues in an effort to promote safety in states that have legalized medical and/or recreational marijuana. This is an area where our fear-based approach to policy has held us back.

At the time of this writing, almost nineteen million Americans had used marijuana last month,[4] yet have you ever heard anyone warn about the dangers of drugged driving? Probably not: even with more people using and driving, we have yet to talk seriously about this vital public safety issue. In fact, the general consensus is that marijuana is not as dangerous as alcohol, and an alarming number of people think that it is completely harmless. Then there are the anti-marijuana crusaders who downplay the data showing that most people who use marijuana do not become addicted to it. They also may, at times, misrepresent research findings about the potential dangers of marijuana, implying that any use of the drug will automatically bring bad outcomes. Marijuana is neither harmless nor evil, but as long as both sides of the debate continue to distort the facts, the real problems will never be addressed.

Widespread use of marijuana for recreational and medical

purposes has led many powerful spokespeople to praise the drug. Numerous athletes and celebrities—even politicians such as President Obama and former President Clinton—have discussed their use of marijuana. Some seem to go out of their way to publicize their use of the drug and their opinions about its safety. Former NFL running back Ricky Williams was candid about his marijuana use and felt that it did not keep him from reaching his athletic potential, telling sportswriters, "I don't agree that it was an Achilles heel, I kind of think of it was more like spinach for Popeye."[5] When celebrities talk about marijuana, more often than not they do so to endorse its use. But there are also some high-profile people who are honest about how using marijuana was harmful to them and who do not recommend it. Lady Gaga recently talked about her marijuana use and stated unequivocally that she found it addictive: "I have been addicted to it and it's ultimately related to anxiety coping and it's a form of self-medication and I was smoking up to 15–20 marijuana cigarettes a day with no tobacco."[6] It seems, however, that for every celebrity warning about the risk of addiction to marijuana, as Lady Gaga did, there are probably five who endorse its use. This may be a reflexive response to the exaggerated negative information about marijuana that was fed to the public for years. Yet this polarized presentation of information is what makes it so difficult to sort out the realities of marijuana and to then craft sensible marijuana health policy.

The Battle for Public Perception

The increased media coverage that tends to promote misperceptions about marijuana may have contributed to the recent 2013 Monitoring the Future data, which shows that, unlike trends for other drugs, use of marijuana among young people is on the rise and, perhaps even more alarming, perception of risk is on the decline.[7] Monitoring the Future is an important annual survey conducted by researchers at the University of Michigan that tracks young people's drug and alcohol use patterns and attitudes. Keeping apprised of rates of marijuana use over time has obvious value, but following perception of risk is very important as well because young people are more likely to try drugs when they do not anticipate being harmed by them. Until recently, this may also explain some of the appeal of prescription drugs and synthetic drugs that flooded the marketplace a few years ago. Several aspects of marijuana use contribute to the ease with which it can be misunderstood, causing young people to downplay its risks. There are two aspects in particular that must be addressed in order to grasp why people have difficulty understanding the data on marijuana, thereby adding to the knowledge gap.

The first reason that marijuana is often misunderstood is because people try to paint the issues related to marijuana with a broad brush. As mentioned above, people often are invested emotionally in a particular side of this debate and therefore tend to oversimplify the issues. This leads to a loss of objectivity and, possibly, a loss of credibility as well. The medical marijuana debate is a great example of this. Those who oppose the use of medical marijuana rarely acknowledge either the therapeutic potential of cannabinoids and the marijuana plant or the desire of many people with significant medical illnesses to find an effective treatment. Conversely, those in favor of medical marijuana fail to recognize the concerns about having medical marijuana end up in the hands of young people and adults vulnerable to addiction, as well as data suggesting that many with medical marijuana certifications do not have debilitating conditions like cancer or AIDS. The result is that a considerable amount of skewed points of view and half-truths are promoted to the public because those at either end of the debate are the ones who talk about it the most to media outlets.

The second most common reason marijuana is often misunderstood is that people can be misguided by their own experiences. Many of us have had personal experiences with the
drug. But if our experiences were decades ago—in the 1960s,
1970s, or even the 1980s, for example—then we may not fully
comprehend all the issues raised by today's marijuana, which
is much stronger than it once was. This is an important factor
as parents make decisions about how to talk to their children
about marijuana. Parents may think that because they smoked
pot when they were younger and they turned out fine, their kids
will be fine if they use it too. The potency of today's marijuana
versus the drug from the 1960s is generally so great, you might
as well be talking about two different drugs. Parents may not
know that the intense high of a drug as strong as today's marijuana raises the ante for the negative impact of the drug, including addiction. It doesn't help that most people aren't likely
to know anyone with an addiction to marijuana. One reason
for that could be that people addicted to marijuana seek treatment even less often than people with other addictions, in part
because society still does not recognize marijuana addiction.
I have seen patients who have spent years abusing marijuana
with the misconception that it isn't addictive get a look of profound relief upon realizing that they aren't "crazy" but have
become addicted to a drug—just as surely as people who have
lost control of their heroin or alcohol use are addicted. And with
that realization comes the dawning of understanding.

Opioids, named for the opium of the poppy plant from
which the first opioid drugs were derived, are compounds like
morphine, oxycodone, OxyContin, hydrocodone (Vicodin), and
many others that are prescribed by physicians as painkillers.
The street drug heroin, originally developed by Bayer, was one
of the first opioids developed and is well known as an addictive, illicit drug. Yet some of the prescription opioids sitting in

medicine cabinets today are far more potent than heroin and are sought after by recreational drug users as well as those who are drug dependent. With people dying every day from opioid and heroin overdoses, it can be difficult to put marijuana use into context. "At least Johnny is not using heroin" is a common thought among parents with children in their teens and early twenties who are using marijuana.

But while marijuana may be less dangerous in many ways than opioids, it is still potentially dangerous. In 2013, I published a study with Dr. Bethany Bracken that underscored why any drug use by a young person, including marijuana use, should be taken very seriously.[8] Our research showed that, among adolescents, progression from marijuana use to marijuana addiction can occur very quickly and that marijuana addiction can progress to addiction of other substances very quickly as well. A few years ago I, perhaps naively, thought that we as clinicians had some time to work with when a young person was first presented for treatment with substance use that had yet to progress to a full-blown addiction. Unfortunately, that has not turned out to be the case. Things can progress very quickly with addiction, especially with a brain that's still developing, and this is why *any* substance use by a young person needs to be taken as seriously as possible.

Peter

Peter, a twenty-eight-year-old lawyer, was doing well as an associate in a high-powered litigation firm downtown. He was in his second year at the firm and had earned a reputation as a solid performer who handled assignments effectively. He worried that he may not be billing enough hours to meet the expectations of his superiors, but overall he felt that things were going well enough for him to be on the path to make partner eventually.

Peter drank alcohol occasionally when out with colleagues or friends, but he had always preferred marijuana to alcohol. From his high school days, he enjoyed the way that he felt calm and pleasantly detached when he smoked. Nothing bothered him when he was "blazed." He smoked daily, at different points throughout the day, during his junior and senior years of high school and smoked regularly, although not quite daily, while at the prestigious Ivy League university several of his family members had attended. His knack for crushing standardized tests had come in handy, but he always did reasonably well in his classes.

These days, he still smoked three or four nights a week—he thought of it like most people thought about drinking. He could not think of a better way to unwind after a twelve-hour day at the firm. While his girlfriend and his mother could not understand why he was still smoking as much as he did, many of his friends from his hometown often talked about how he was someone who smoked a lot and still was highly successful.

Young people can be misled by their own experiences as well. While any exposure they have to marijuana is to today's strong marijuana, young people can misjudge the dangers of the drug based on the experiences of celebrities or their peers. When a young person ends up in my office for a consultation, often at the strong urging of their parents, I frequently hear stories such as "my friend Liz is doing well at Harvard, and she has smoked every day for years" or comparable examples of successful artists or athletes who use marijuana regularly. Such examples, like the case study above, clearly exist.

Peter's case shows another way in which the gray areas around marijuana present themselves. Does his marijuana use rise to the level of a disorder and is he in need of treatment? It is hard to know based on the limited information presented, but there are many key issues raised in Peter's situation. He is unquestionably a talented individual with a track record of academic and professional success. And yes, it's true that many successful people use marijuana. Of course, this does not mean that they are successful *because* of their marijuana use. Nor does it mean that they are successful *in spite* of their marijuana use. Not all marijuana use is the same: the amount and pattern of use is important as you consider individual cases.

With respect to Peter's level of achievement, the question becomes whether or not he is fulfilling his potential. It appears that Peter reduced his use from daily in high school to the three to four times a week he uses currently. He was able to smoke throughout the day in high school, but he limited his use to the evenings as he advanced to more challenging academic and professional environments. Whether people are aware of it or not, the margin for error—what someone is able to "get away with"—gets smaller and smaller as one rises through the ranks and takes on more demanding responsibilities. Peter always performed extremely well on standardized tests, but perhaps his classroom performances were not on par with his testing. This discrepancy begs the question of whether his frequent marijuana use affected his day-to-day performance in a subtle way that was not captured on the standardized tests.

Peter does not appear to be addicted to marijuana. He may have qualified for a mild to moderate marijuana use disorder (using the *DSM-5* criteria, which also includes "severe") during high school when he was using frequently throughout the day, but using three to four times a week, only in the evenings, without pronounced problems related to work, school, or family is not likely to meet psychiatric criteria for marijuana addiction. If he had been evaluated during high school and asked probing questions to determine how his daily marijuana use was affecting other areas of his life, there is a good chance that the evaluation would have revealed that his use was negatively affecting other important areas of his life. However, reducing his use as he progressed to college seemed to be an adaptive maneuver that lessened the potential for problems related to his use.

His current use does not appear to be different from how a typical twenty-eight-year-old would use alcohol. Occasional use of marijuana or alcohol, while making an effort to minimize risk by avoiding driving, for example, carries limited potential for negative consequences. And although Peter's use during high school and college, while his brain was still developing, carried more risks for cognitive impairment, his current use likely does not pose the same risks. It is noteworthy that multiple people close to him—his girlfriend and mother in this case—expressed concern about his marijuana use. This alone would be enough to encourage some people to seek an evaluation from an addiction professional. However, while there are certainly healthier ways to relax after a hard day at work, such as exercise, overall it does not appear that Peter's use would qualify as marijuana addiction. People who use in the manner that Peter uses marijuana usually do not end up ever seeing a health professional about their marijuana use.

In any situation where someone has used marijuana regularly for an extended period of time without apparent negative consequences, there are two issues that should be considered. First, for every marijuana "success" story like Peter's, there are many other cases where the user either struggles mightily or, upon closer examination, may actually be experiencing problems related to the same level of marijuana use. It is difficult, after all, for most people to admit that they are not doing as well as they would like to be. Again, it is important to emphasize that it is regular (daily or nearly everyday) use that we're talking about here. From my clinical experience with patients, it is unlikely, although not impossible, to use marijuana regularly without encountering difficulties in important areas of your life.

The other issue to consider is the margin for error. Immensely talented individuals may be able to get away with regular marijuana use more easily than those of us with more modest talents. The margin for error, even for those with supreme talents, gets smaller and smaller as people progress, climbing the ladder in their respective careers. This is one way that people with marijuana problems end up in treatment—they are not as successful at their current position as they had been in the past, and they wonder if their marijuana use is holding them back. This is a key question to consider, and most regular users do consider it at some point. Are they performing at their highest level, and, if not, is their marijuana use playing a role in their inability to reach their goals? This is a challenging question and, even when people ultimately conclude that their marijuana use has become an impediment, it is still difficult to change a behavior that they have engaged in for years. And if someone is truly addicted, quitting without help is very difficult.

Situations like Peter's show the gray areas associated with marijuana use and marijuana policy. The murky, undefined areas in Peter's situation extend beyond the question of how much his marijuana use has affected his job performance. Social policies are in play here as well. Peter is a lawyer who regularly chooses to use an illegal drug. Does this mean that he is a criminal? Consider how he would be treated in comparison to a colleague who chose to consume copious quantities of alcohol every evening, perhaps even getting charged with multiple driving while intoxicated (DWI) infractions. If his colleague was able to get his DWI charges dropped, he is not considered a criminal. But one can argue that Peter *is* a criminal based on federal law defining marijuana as an illegal drug. One might also consider whether Peter should be disbarred due to his tendency to use an illegal drug.

Is Peter blatantly disregarding the law or is he simply reflecting a common belief—that laws related to marijuana do not reflect reality. The latter seems more likely here, especially considering that former U.S. attorney general Eric Holder repeatedly expressed a desire to let states decide how to handle marijuana-related policies.[9] But if we condone Peter's regular use of an illegal, potentially addictive substance, are we increasing the odds that more people will use marijuana like Peter does, thereby increasing the number of people who may ultimately develop marijuana addiction? These are important, yet complex questions to consider.

Peter's situation also foreshadows tricky issues that are raised in the marijuana legalization debate. There is a point where personal behavior becomes a concern of society, but it is hard to know where that point is. Most would argue that marijuana use, while currently illegal on a federal level, is not a public concern if it's limited to the confines of one's home. There are other examples of society looking the other way on issues of legality depending on circumstances. For example, jaywalking when there is no traffic around is unlikely to draw a citation, but jaywalking in heavy traffic is a safety issue that will provoke a citation. We should be concerned about people driving vehicles under the influence of marijuana, but it is much more difficult to determine precisely when marijuana use affects performance at an office job. If taxpayers are paying the salaries of government workers who are underperforming due to marijuana use, then I imagine that some of us would not be happy about it.

These questions underline a common American conundrum: the tug-of-war between morality instilled for many in Puritan or Calvinist times and Libertarian doctrine that favors personal freedom to do whatever we choose, even if it is harmful to us.

Summary

In this first chapter, we covered lots of ground, from the basics of the science of marijuana to its fascinating history to the many reasons that it is misunderstood by so many people. Marijuana is a plant that has tremendous medical potential and, like other substances with important medical uses, its misuse can result in harm and negative consequences. I urged you in the first chapter to embrace the gray areas of marijuana: it is not entirely good or entirely bad, and overly simplistic arguments that promote these ideas should be rejected as lacking credibility. The science and history of marijuana are a great place to start learning the truth about marijuana because they demonstrate that very little about the drug is simple. Peter's situation in our case study—regular marijuana use by a professional who seems to be performing well—illustrates this and provides a glimpse into the types of complex issues associated with marijuana. The science, the history, and the reasons that marijuana is often misunderstood are all areas that must be addressed and grasped in order to progress to the other difficult and nuanced topics described in later chapters.

2

A Small Fraction of a Large Number Can Be a Very Large Number

For all of the talk about marijuana—especially with the issues of medical marijuana and legalization of marijuana being raised in state after state—we do not hear enough about the *numbers* related to marijuana use. Without knowing these numbers, it is impossible to grasp the scope of the issue and how many people marijuana policies will affect.

How we get our news these days has a lot to do with the challenges we have understanding and making sense of the issues surrounding marijuana. Often, young people do not read newspapers, even online newspapers, and they hear about things from friends or from short blasts of information on television shows like *The Daily Show with Jon Stewart*, through social media platforms like Twitter, or on websites like Tumblr or reddit. These sources tend to gloss over the numbers related to marijuana, perhaps due to space limitations. This is curious, because the popularity of marijuana drives not only the media's focus on it but the epidemiology, or statistics, of marijuana use as well. Thus, young people get a lot of their information about marijuana from sources that often fail to address the scope of the issues.

This patchy information system works, at different times, to the advantage of either pro- or anti-marijuana advocates, who may downplay certain statistics to bolster their arguments for or against marijuana. The result is often a presentation skewed toward an agenda-driven perspective.

Some people will recall that there was an active misinformation campaign regarding another smokable herb—tobacco. It is worth pointing out that the difficulty in getting all the facts about marijuana, including the statistics, is different from misinformation that has been spread in the past about cigarettes. The Big Tobacco companies deliberately misled potential customers in the 1950s in an attempt to hide the truth about the addictiveness and other health risks of nicotine. Fortunately, large corporations have not been involved (at least, so far) in marketing marijuana, although we will discuss this possibility in chapter 6 when we cover the pros and cons of legalizing recreational marijuana. The current gap between the science and public perception of marijuana most likely is not a deliberate creation, as it was with tobacco, but rather an unfortunate outcome of an informal word-of-mouth campaign.

The result is that far too few people grasp the scientific facts about marijuana. While we explore the science of marijuana in this book in great detail with a goal of separating the myths from the facts, understanding the drug's epidemiology—the statistics about *who* uses, *how much* they use, and *why* they use— will help you put the importance of the issue into perspective.

To put the scope of marijuana use into sharper focus, let's look at the statistics regarding the use of other drugs. According to the National Survey of Drug Use and Health, more than 82 percent (eight out of ten) of Americans age twelve or older have used alcohol at some point in their lifetime.[10] More than 61 percent (six out of ten) in that age group have smoked cigarettes during their lifetime. Among illicit drugs, marijuana is the most commonly used substance in the United States by a wide

margin, with more than 47 percent (close to five out of ten) of
Americans age twelve or older having used marijuana during
their lifetime. Now consider the use rates for other illicit drugs
that we hear about frequently: for cocaine, methamphetamine,
and heroin, the percentage of Americans who have used in the
past year is 14.7 percent, 4.6 percent, and 1.6 percent, respectively. (That means that more than one out of ten people have
used cocaine, one out of twenty have used meth, and one out
of fifty have used heroin.) Prescription pain reliever misuse has
been on the rise lately, but still only 13.3 percent of Americans
age twelve or older have used these drugs to get high in their
lifetime, about the same rate as cocaine. In sum, marijuana use
lags behind the use of the legal substances alcohol and tobacco,
but it dwarfs the use of other illicit drugs.[11] As pointed out in
chapter 1, almost nineteen million Americans used marijuana
in the past month. According to 2010 U.S. census figures, that is
roughly equal to the number of residents in the state of Florida.
Figure 1 on the next page shows the relative numbers of people
using these substances.

Marijuana math can be tricky. Many of us do not like to do
math problems with large numbers, and the numbers related to
marijuana use are quite large: More people use marijuana than
any other illicit drug, not just in America, but worldwide.[12] In
fact, other illicit drugs don't even come close. This large number of users underscores the importance of the policies we are
crafting relative to marijuana decriminalization, medical use,
and legalization. These policies affect the millions of marijuana
users. But remember, they also affect the many more millions of
people who interact with users. There are many controversial
issues with emotional, poignant aspects that affect small groups
of people, but that is not the case here. Marijuana affects most
of us, so it is important to try to get the policies right.

FIGURE 1. Lifetime use of mood-altering drugs

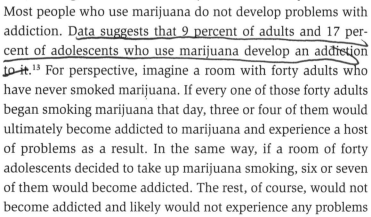

All people	
People who have used alcohol	
People who have used nicotine (cigarettes)	
People who have used marijuana	
People who have used cocaine	
People who have used prescription pain relievers to get high	
People who have used meth	
People who have used heroin	

Putting Addiction to Marijuana into Perspective

Most people who use marijuana do not develop problems with addiction. Data suggests that 9 percent of adults and 17 percent of adolescents who use marijuana develop an addiction to it.[13] For perspective, imagine a room with forty adults who have never smoked marijuana. If every one of those forty adults began smoking marijuana that day, three or four of them would ultimately become addicted to marijuana and experience a host of problems as a result. In the same way, if a room of forty adolescents decided to take up marijuana smoking, six or seven of them would become addicted. The rest, of course, would not become addicted and likely would not experience any problems associated with their marijuana use. Put simply, this data tells us that most people who begin using marijuana will not become addicted, but some will. And adolescents are about twice as likely as adults to become addicted. We should think a little more about these numbers, though. At first glance, 9 percent may not seem like a very large number. If only four out of forty adults will develop problems with addiction that will adversely affect their lives, that seems like a small fraction of the room. Well, if that room were filled with forty of your closest family and friends, would you want to take the risk that four of them will develop a serious problem that will contribute to major difficulties in many important areas of their lives? To look at it another way, imagine you are on a racetrack, zipping around the oval at high speeds with forty other drivers, and four of them are under the influence of marijuana. Is that a risk you would like to take? This question will be relevant to our discussion of legalizing marijuana in chapter 6.

To fully understand marijuana, we must know both its relative addictiveness in comparison to other drugs and the number of people who become addicted. Only considering one side of these numbers can lead you astray. Some research has shown that the percentage of users becoming addicted to nicotine, heroin, cocaine, and alcohol was 32 percent, 23 percent, 17 percent, and 15 percent, respectively.[14] At a rate of 9 percent (for adults), marijuana is less addictive than these substances. But it is important that we avoid making the leap that is often made—that is, thinking that marijuana is *not addictive*. It is *less* addictive than these other commonly used and abused substances, but it *is* potentially addictive. It's also important to remember that though addiction affects one person, the person who is addicted isn't on a desert island. He or she affects many other people.

What's more, the total number of Americans with marijuana addiction is quite significant, because a small fraction of a large

number can be a very large number. The result is that 2.7 million Americans meet criteria for marijuana addiction. *That's
equivalent to every resident of the city of Houston, Texas, being
addicted to marijuana.* It can be difficult to wrap our heads
around this fact due to the somewhat abstract nature of large
numbers, and because we don't often hear about those addicted
to marijuana. So, while most people who use marijuana don't
become addicted to it, the small fraction who do happen to develop an addiction total more than 2.7 million people, and for
these people, their marijuana use is a very serious problem. If
you're like most people, this may be surprising news. We typically don't hear about these addicted people and their problems
because of the public perception that marijuana is harmless
and not addictive. Furthermore, most people with addiction
to any drug (alcohol, cocaine, and so on) do not seek treatment, and those with marijuana addiction are even *less* likely
to seek treatment when they are bombarded with the message
that marijuana is not addictive. "Why am I struggling to stop
using marijuana if it is not addictive?" they wonder. As we will
see later when we take a closer look at marijuana's addictive
properties, these people are often relieved to understand what's
behind their struggle.

Considering the substantial number of people who use
marijuana and become addicted, it is puzzling that we hear
more about the potential dangers of opioid use than the risk of
addiction to marijuana. This is especially true when we consider that the number of Americans affected by marijuana is so
much greater than the number affected by opioids, including
heroin. The same holds true for methamphetamine and other
illicit drug use. Part of this imbalance may be due to the insidious, or slow-developing, nature of the effects of marijuana
addiction. When treating those with addictions, we usually do
not see people come into treatment for marijuana addiction as

a result of catastrophic events. It is true that no one overdoses on marijuana like they do on opioids. And yet, like those with addictions to other drugs, people with marijuana problems experience difficulties in work, school, or relationships connected to their drug use. This tends to be overlooked because these problems often develop over months or years of the person ignoring more and more responsibilities in order to spend more time smoking marijuana.

Summary

We have spent chapter 2 diving into the complex statistics and ideas surrounding marijuana use. Many of the statistics related to marijuana are not intuitive—some objective, critical thinking is required in order to fully grasp them. This is part of the process of becoming comfortable in the gray areas of marijuana, somewhere between the extremes of "Marijuana is an evil drug that is as bad as heroin or cocaine" and "Marijuana is completely harmless and should be available to whoever wants it." We learned that marijuana is the most commonly used illicit drug in the world and in the United States in particular. As a result, the policies we craft related to decriminalization of marijuana, medical marijuana, and legalization of marijuana affect millions—both the people who use marijuana and those affected by the behavior of these users. Many people, however, will downplay these numbers and point out that most people who use marijuana do not become addicted to it, that it is not as addictive as many of the other drugs we are familiar with, such as opioids or cocaine and legal drugs like alcohol and nicotine. Keep in mind that just because marijuana is less addictive than some other drugs does not mean it is not addictive or not potentially dangerous. The statistics tell us that the seemingly small percentage of people addicted to marijuana actually translates into millions of addicts in the United States—about the same number as the population of Houston, Texas—simply because of the sheer number of users. With so many people using marijuana, the impact of marijuana use is vast, with major social and financial implications. Because of marijuana's wide-ranging influence, it is critical to understand how it works, its appeal, the pros and cons of using it, and how policies that regulate its use might affect us. In order to understand marijuana and to continue to bridge the gap between science and public perception, we will now move on from the statistics of use to explore three of the most commonly held myths about marijuana. For years these myths have been contributing to the information gap about the impact of this drug.

SECTION II
THE THREE MYTHS

CHAPTER

3

MYTH #1

Marijuana Is Not Harmful

Most people today do not consider marijuana to be a harmful
drug like heroin, cocaine, or methamphetamine. Our perception
of marijuana is colored by our own experiences—and many of
us have had experiences with marijuana without major consequences. We are not alone. As noted in the previous chapter,
just 9 percent of adults and 17 percent of adolescents will develop an addiction to marijuana.[15]

The Harmful Effects of Marijuana Use

~~Problems are much more likely to arise if someone uses~~ mar-
~~ijuana daily or nearly every day, or if someone begins~~ regular
~~use as an adolescent.~~ Occasional use of marijuana is unlikely
to be harmful in the same way that drinking in moderation is
unlikely to be harmful. I can go out on a Saturday night and
drink four glasses of wine over the course of four hours or so,
have my wife drive home, and my drinking is not likely to cause
problems. The same holds true for occasional marijuana use.
When people begin to smoke marijuana multiple times a week,
however, they often continue on to daily or near-daily smoking,
and that's when the problems begin.

Regular use—daily or nearly every day—often leads to marijuana addiction. "Addiction"—use that qualifies as a marijuana use disorder—means repeated use despite harm. According to the American Psychiatric Association's most recent *Diagnostic and Statistical Manual of Mental Disorders (DSM-5)*, those who have a marijuana use disorder continue to use marijuana although their marijuana use has already caused major problems in many important areas of their lives, such as in school, work, or relationships. As noted earlier, there are 2.7 million Americans who are addicted to marijuana right now who could benefit from treatment. That large number is probably why our research team does not have much difficulty recruiting participants for our studies to develop treatments for marijuana addiction. Catastrophic events—overdoses, assaults, arrests—are often what lead people into treatment for the "hard drugs." No one fatally overdoses on marijuana, and dramatic events rarely lead people to get treatment for their marijuana use. Problems from marijuana tend to creep up gradually—someone may not be performing well at work or may be withdrawing from loved ones in order to spend more and more time smoking. Regular use of marijuana can affect many aspects of the lives of users and their loved ones. Patients routinely come to see me to help them stop using marijuana because they are on the verge of getting kicked out of school or fired from their job. Excellent scientific research shows that regular marijuana use affects the ability to think, can increase feelings of anxiety and depression, and increases the odds that one will develop psychotic disorders such as schizophrenia.

Effects of marijuana on thinking

Your brain cannot perform the way it is supposed to when you use marijuana. Few will argue that their brains can function at a high level when they are "blazed"—feeling the mind-altering effects of marijuana. The main active ingredient in the drug is delta-9-tetrahydrocannabinol, or THC, which produces the high. Marijuana growers use the latest technology to produce varieties of marijuana with as much THC as possible in an attempt to appeal to marijuana users who want the most powerful marijuana they can get. THC affects the body when it plugs into microscopic sockets in the brain called "cannabinoid receptors." Many of these receptors are found in the parts of the brain that control thinking, concentration, coordination, and memory. The short-term effects of marijuana use include increased heart rate, slowed reaction time (which can double the risk of being involved in a car accident), and coordination and balance problems.[16] These short-term effects can result in marijuana users getting into trouble.

But the long-term effects of regular marijuana use are even more troublesome. Several research studies have shown that regular marijuana use hinders frontal-executive brain function, the ability to perform tasks that require complex thinking. In real life, an example of a task that requires complex thinking is riding a bike on a roadway shared with cars and pedestrians— this calls for skills associated with riding a bike as well as skills to safely negotiate traffic and other potential hazards. In one such study conducted by Dr. Staci Gruber, a colleague of mine at McLean Hospital, chronic marijuana smokers and nonsmokers each performed a series of neurocognitive tests that measure how well the brain is working.[17] The marijuana smokers in this study smoked five or more days per week, they had smoked at least 2,500 times in their lives, and they met the conditions necessary to have a diagnosis of marijuana addiction. These conditions include needing more and more marijuana to get the same effect once produced by a smaller amount, spending lots of time trying to get more marijuana, and choosing to smoke marijuana instead of attending family events and activities— all diagnostic criteria for a marijuana use disorder in *DSM-5*.

The neurocognitive tests consisted of an IQ test and several other tests that included drawing, pattern recognition, verbal tasks, and word tests, all designed to carefully assess a variety of ways that we routinely ask our brain to learn. Such tests include separating objects or words that meet specific criteria from many that do not meet the criteria, as well as following directions in an effort to solve puzzles. The marijuana smokers performed much worse than the nonsmokers on several of these tests.

Among the marijuana smokers, those who began smoking marijuana regularly before age sixteen performed especially poorly on the tests. This study also showed that those who began smoking marijuana regularly before age sixteen smoked twice as often and nearly three times as much marijuana per week compared to the marijuana smokers who began smoking later in life—which indicates increased tolerance, another key criterion for addiction.

Another study by Dr. Gruber's group demonstrated that those who began smoking regularly had to use different parts of their brains than nonsmokers to complete certain tests.[18] The long-term meaning of these studies is not clear, but what is clear is that the brains of marijuana smokers need to work harder than the brains of nonsmokers in order to keep up. A recent study called into question whether even occasional use of marijuana affects a user's brain in a negative way. This study showed that occasional marijuana use was associated with changes in size of key brain structures.[19] While we cannot say reliably from one study that occasional marijuana use affects the development of key brain structures, this study makes this a question that requires further research.

While regular marijuana use at any age can cause serious problems, use among those age sixteen or younger is especially worrisome because of the increased likelihood of addiction to marijuana and the potential long-term consequences on brain development. While we don't want kids to use marijuana at all, the research shows this is one party that it is better for teens to be late to—or to skip altogether!

Other studies show that regular marijuana use also causes your IQ to drop. A recent study by Duke University researcher Dr. Madeline Meier and her colleagues followed more than 1,000 New Zealand residents over their lifetimes, measuring their scores on IQ tests at ages thirteen and thirty-eight.[20] IQ measures one's overall intelligence potential more than performance and, therefore, it should not change much over time. The researchers wanted to see if marijuana use might affect that potential. The Gruber study I referred to earlier looked at brain performance over the short term, while the Meier study looked at brain potential over a lifetime. The results confirmed what many feared. Regular marijuana use beginning in the teenage years led to a general decline in IQ. Those who used marijuana regularly for years experienced about an eight-point drop in their IQ scores over a twenty-five-year period. Eight points could be the difference between an above-average IQ and an average one—or an average IQ and a below-average one. Not only did regular marijuana use limit the potential of the brain to perform at a high level, but actually stopping marijuana use for periods of more than a year *did not allow IQ levels to return to normal.* This important study showed us that early, regular use of marijuana had lasting, irreversible effects on the brain—a "point of no return" exists.

More than half of the patients coming into our program for treatment of other drug problems describe a time in their lives, usually in their late teens and early twenties, when they smoked marijuana regularly, often daily, for a period of years. What if this regular use could be prevented or if we could intervene in these young people's lives with treatments that help them stop using marijuana? I have to believe that we would dramatically reduce the number of people who end up in treatment for problems with alcohol or other drugs.

Effects of marijuana on anxiety

The link between marijuana and anxiety is another reason that so many people become addicted to the drug. Among the patients I have treated for marijuana problems in a variety of settings—in the hospital, my private practice, and in my clinical research studies—anxiety is among the top three reasons that people continue to use marijuana (enhancing recreational activities and poor sleep are the other two). In order to treat marijuana problems, clinicians must constantly be thinking about what other problems a patient may be having. Almost three out of every four marijuana users (72 percent) also have a psychiatric problem like anxiety or depression. Marijuana is the most commonly used illicit drug in the world, and anxiety is the most common psychiatric problem in the world.[21] Considering those facts, it is not hard to see why it is crucial to understand the relationship between the two.

Marijuana can worsen anxiety in two key ways. It can worsen generalized feelings of anxiety, and it can cause panic attacks. *Generalized* anxiety is anxiety that occurs for no particular reason. It includes symptoms such as worrying excessively and constantly about things that are unlikely to happen and feeling tense or anxious all day for no reason. The experience is mentally and physically exhausting. Generalized anxiety can worsen as the effects of marijuana are wearing off.[22]

Panic attacks are frightening events that usually include shortness of breath, a "racing" heart, dizziness or weakness, the sensation of a loss of control, and the feeling that something very bad is about to happen. Panic attacks can occur when a person has been exposed to a high dose of marijuana, either through smoking or by eating marijuana that is very strong, or potent, due to the high concentration of THC. One of the concerns about medical marijuana becoming more available in the United States is that it will mean people will have easier access to more potent marijuana. And the more people who are using stronger, more potent marijuana, the more users who will be likely to experience anxiety and frightening panic attacks.

Marijuana's effect on generalized feelings of anxiety is a critical topic; I discuss it with every patient with marijuana problems. Generalized anxiety may be present for long stretches of the day. It may become worse when a person thinks about a stressful situation, but these generalized feelings are not a response to an incident or thought; they just happen, kind of like a bad mood. Marijuana can affect these feelings of anxiety in a deeper way, producing what is referred to in the field of medicine as a "rebound effect" (see figure 2). For example, a person will have feelings of anxiety, smoke marijuana in response to those feelings, and then experience a decline in anxiety level. So when people report feeling less anxious, or even mellow, after smoking marijuana, they are usually right. The problem begins, however, when the effects of the marijuana wear off. When the marijuana

FIGURE 2. Marijuana and anxiety

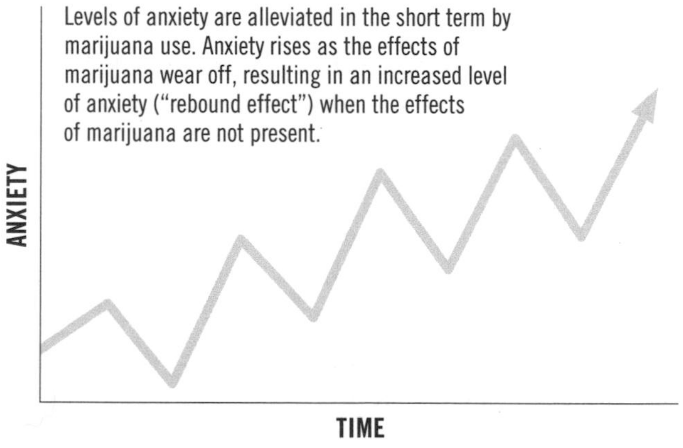

Levels of anxiety are alleviated in the short term by marijuana use. Anxiety rises as the effects of marijuana wear off, resulting in an increased level of anxiety ("rebound effect") when the effects of marijuana are not present.

ANXIETY

TIME

wears off, the anxiety level creeps up again, often to a level that is greater than the original feelings.

While people may have periods without generalized anxiety, they will likely experience these feelings of anxiety if they use marijuana regularly and the effects eventually wear off. These people end up digging a hole of sorts: their baseline level of anxiety—the level of anxiety felt *without* marijuana—climbs higher and higher in a rebound response to marijuana. Stopping use of marijuana altogether is the best way to treat these growing feelings of anxiety, but it is very difficult for patients to believe this advice because they know that marijuana use, at least in the short term, makes their anxiety better. The fact is, they are likely to be addicted to marijuana, as they've come to rely on it to avoid these terrible feelings of anxiety.

Rich

Rich was a fifty-two-year-old, single, manual laborer with a past medical history of anxiety who came to me to help him stop smoking marijuana. He had been smoking marijuana for more than thirty years, and he had been smoking daily for the past eight years. He described feeling anxious "all the time" for a variety of reasons. He had been prescribed two different antidepressants in the past but, he said, "They didn't work so I only took them for a few weeks."

Rich would wake up feeling anxious and he would feel this way for most of the day. He managed these feelings by smoking marijuana four to six times per day; he smoked within fifteen minutes of waking up in the morning, then one or two times during the workday when he would take breaks in his truck, then immediately upon arriving home, and finally one or two more times before retiring in the evening. He knew that he "was smoking too much" and that "it probably was not helping" him, and he had tried to stop before without success.

Those attempts led to feelings of even worse anxiety, irritability, and some trouble sleeping.

Rich and I worked through a ten-week program of cognitive behavioral therapy (CBT) aimed at examining the thoughts, feelings, and behaviors surrounding his marijuana use. We talked in great detail about each of the situations in which he smoked marijuana. How did he feel before he went to sit in his truck and smoke? How did he feel afterward and how long did that feeling last? Were there times when he could not smoke during the workday because he was too busy or because he did not have marijuana? Were there other ways that he managed anxiety in those instances when he could not smoke?

It turns out that Rich was paired up occasionally with a co-worker who did not smoke marijuana, and they would take breaks together. Rich was not comfortable smoking around this co-worker; instead they spent their breaks discussing their shared interest in music. Rich was able to recognize that when he was paired with this co-worker, he was not anxious throughout the day and that he worked just fine, even though he would not smoke marijuana during that particular workday. In our treatment, we used this realization to fuel thoughts that he really did not need marijuana to manage these feelings of anxiety. He cut his smoking in half after three weeks of treatment and by week ten he had almost completely stopped.

Not everyone achieves this level of success in treatment for marijuana addiction. Many struggle to reduce their use at all, and some revert back to the way they smoked prior to treatment. But Rich's case shows the importance of the relationship between marijuana and anxiety. It also shows how cognitive behavioral therapy can work to help motivated people reduce their smoking or stop altogether. Cognitive behavioral therapy is a form of counseling in which a person examines the interaction of thoughts, feelings, and behaviors. The client explores how patterns of thinking lead to self-destructive actions, and then finds ways to change these patterns. Doing weekly CBT can be very hard work, and many people would rather not invest their time and money to do this type of talk therapy. Rich was fed up after multiple attempts on his own to stop using marijuana, so he made a serious effort to seek and participate in treatment that led to excellent results.

Rich's case reveals several things. First, it shows the myth of marijuana's harmlessness to be just that—a myth. Second, it reveals that people may develop an addiction to marijuana while trying to address symptoms of anxiety that are bothering them. Finally, Rich's case shows that once someone's marijuana use is identified as a problem, there are treatments available that can help the person either significantly cut down on use or stop altogether.

Effects of marijuana on depression

Marijuana use has long been associated with "amotivational syndrome." This condition is marked by a lack of energy, poor motivation, and withdrawal from social situations. While the research supporting this association has not been strong, aspects of this syndrome have been observed in many patients who have marijuana addiction. Interestingly, problems with energy, motivation, and social withdrawal are also seen in depressed people. A recent analysis of studies looking at the relationship between marijuana use and depression showed that heavy marijuana use, the level of use typically seen in those with marijuana addiction, was in fact associated with depression.[23] So while we know that those who use marijuana regularly are more likely to suffer from depression than those who do not, we do not know if marijuana use causes depression or if being depressed leads people to smoke more.

From a clinical perspective, the "which came first—chicken or egg?" argument about marijuana addiction and depression is less important than the fact that clinicians and family members need to be aware that these serious problems often occur at the same time. I ask questions about depressive symptoms like decreased energy, poor appetite, hopelessness, lack of enjoyment in daily activities, and erratic sleep every time I see a patient with marijuana addiction in my office. More important, since people battling depression are more likely than those without depression to think about suicide, I ask blunt, to-the-point questions about suicide during every office visit as well.

Effects of marijuana on the development of psychosis

Stories of marijuana users experiencing psychotic symptoms like hallucinations are common. Many people know others who have suffered bad experiences with marijuana, such periods of time where they described hearing voices or feeling that they were "outside of their body." These hallucinations can be short lived and go away on their own, or they can be the beginning of a lifetime of problems with these symptoms. The acute, or short-lived, psychotic episodes are frightening experiences that often contribute to a person making a decision not to use marijuana again. While no one wants to have a bad experience—even a short one—with marijuana, it is the increased risk of developing a permanent psychotic illness like schizophrenia that has drawn considerable attention from the medical community.

Marijuana use is associated with an increased risk for psychotic disorders like schizophrenia, and recent research has added to our understanding of this relationship. A study by Dr. Rebecca Kuepper and her colleagues in the Netherlands followed a large group of Germans for ten years and found that those who used marijuana were more likely to have short-term episodes of psychotic symptoms and also develop psychotic symptoms that did not go away when compared with people who did not use marijuana.[24] These findings were supported by work done by Dr. Matthew Large's team in Australia. Dr. Large and his colleagues reviewed eighty-three studies that looked at the relationship between substance use and the age at which someone first experienced psychotic symptoms.[25] They found that people who used marijuana and developed psychosis experienced psychotic symptoms earlier than those who did not use marijuana and developed psychosis. The group of substance users who developed psychosis included a large number of marijuana users, and the large proportion of marijuana users in this group suggests that marijuana use causes psychotic symptoms in some people. The take-home message from these important studies is that marijuana use makes it more likely that one will develop either short- or long-term psychotic symptoms.

Summary

As we have seen throughout this chapter, marijuana use can be harmful and lead to problems in multiple areas of your life. It can affect your ability to think, be associated with depression, and increase anxiety or the risk for developing psychosis. Just like the use of "hard drugs" like heroin and cocaine, marijuana use can cause harm. Regular use leads to a psychological and physical addiction that can make it very difficult to stop using, and problems will continue to build up over time.

The result is that, by the time patients are sitting across from me in my office seeking treatment for marijuana addiction, they often have the same types of problems in work, school, and relationships that those addicted to heroin and cocaine have. As the case of Rich shows, these problems can be addressed successfully in treatment. But first the true extent of the problem has to be recognized.

MYTH #2

Marijuana Use Cannot Lead to Addiction

On a handful of occasions each year, I find myself in meetings with doctors from other specialties. At each of these meetings, we begin by going around the room describing, in a few sentences, who we are and what we do. I always mention that I am an addiction psychiatrist who conducts research in hopes of finding a medication to treat marijuana addiction. While that introduction does not produce audible gasps, one or more of these doctors will invariably come up to me at a break in the proceedings and say "Marijuana? I thought that wasn't addictive."

When I first heard other doctors say that they thought marijuana was not addictive, I was surprised. Over the years, however, I have come to realize that these doctors are simply reflecting a common myth about marijuana: that its use cannot lead to addiction. As we learned earlier, marijuana *is* potentially addictive—9 percent of adults and 17 percent of adolescents who use in the United States develop an addiction, resulting in 2.7 million Americans meeting criteria today for marijuana addiction. Causing addiction usually means causing harm, so understanding how marijuana use can lead to marijuana addiction in some people is important because this myth reinforces the first marijuana myth that we discussed in chapter 3: "Marijuana is not harmful."

Because people usually don't think of marijuana in the same way as they think of "hard drugs," they often make the leap to assuming that marijuana is not harmful at all. The science, however, suggests that marijuana—considered a "soft drug" by many—has much in common with hard drugs known for their addictive qualities. In this chapter, I will show how marijuana can be addictive for some people—causing problems in multiple areas of life—and that marijuana addiction is a brain disease that is expressed as a compulsive behavior.

Jason

Jason is a twenty-year-old young man who responded to an advertisement for one of our marijuana addiction clinical trials. He first smoked marijuana at age twelve and was smoking daily by fourteen. "Everyone smokes in my neighborhood," he lamented. He now smoked around three times a day, as he had done for years; he would start by "waking and baking," smoking marijuana within thirty minutes of waking up. He responded to the advertisement because his girlfriend was pregnant and he "didn't want to end up like my father, who is a bad alcoholic." In high school, he did not think about going to college, but with a baby on the way he wondered about stopping marijuana use and taking some classes at the local community college. He said that he knew his smoking was "not healthy" and he thought that he would not be able to do as well as possible in his college classes if he were still smoking every day. He had tried to stop "two or three times before," but those attempts lasted less than a day each time. The last time he tried to stop was a few weeks ago, and he reported that he felt "edgy and couldn't get to sleep by the evening of the first day" and "the day was not going well so I just smoked."

Key Factors in Marijuana Addiction

Historical (genetic), environmental, and physiological factors all play a role in whether someone will become addicted to marijuana.

Historical (genetic) factors

Historical factors encompass both family history, including a family history of addiction, and previous experiences with drugs and alcohol. Addiction is a chronic medical illness like asthma, diabetes, or high blood pressure. These chronic medical illnesses have a genetic component, which explains why you are at higher risk for having addiction problems if someone in your family struggled with addiction, compared with someone with no family history of addiction.[26] For example, Jason is at higher risk for developing an addiction because his father is addicted to alcohol.

"Heritability" refers to the proportion of the observable trait (addiction in this case) that can be attributed to inherited genetic factors as opposed to environmental factors, such as the kind of neighborhood in which you live. While different research studies report varying proportions of heritability linked to genetic factors and environmental factors, one study conducted in 2007 showed that genetic factors accounted for 35 percent (about one-third) of the heritability of marijuana addiction and environmental factors accounted for 47 percent (about one-half).[27] That's just one study, of course. Looking over a variety of studies, we can conclude that researchers have agreed that genes play a role in marijuana addiction, but they have not agreed on how large that role is. Your environment (family behaviors, schools, friends, neighborhood, and other "external" factors) also plays a role. Jason's neighborhood, where he reported that "everyone" seemed to be using marijuana, probably increased the likelihood that he would begin using marijuana on a daily basis.

You are *not* doomed if you have genes for addiction from your family, but if you have a family history of addiction, and therefore genes for addiction, you do need to be more careful about your exposure to alcohol or other drugs. So, for example, working in environments with easy access to drugs or alcohol—such as bars, pharmacies, or hospitals—may not be the healthiest choices if you have a family history of addiction. Similarly, having friends who use mood-altering substances more than most people makes it more likely that you will "express" your addiction genes and get into trouble.

The genes for addiction seem to have a strong pull, affecting many choices people make and behaviors in which they engage. Based purely on observations in my clinical work, it seems that, at times, those with addiction are drawn to situations that place them at risk. I have treated numerous patients with addiction who have chosen at one point or another to work as a bartender, a risky job for someone with a history of addiction. Making bad decisions like this is often due to *impulsivity*, a person's tendency to make quick decisions before thinking them through. Research on impulsivity shows that it is more common in patients with addiction than in people who do not suffer from addiction. In addition, being under the influence of substances makes it more likely that you will make an impulsive decision that you might not otherwise make. (Most of the chemicals people use to get intoxicated or high have a side effect of relaxing judgment—making us vulnerable to poor or impulsive decision-making.) Usually decisions about where to work or who to be friends with are not impulsive decisions. But even with time to think through the options before them, those with addiction can make regrettable choices.

All drug addictions have a genetic component that is passed from generation to generation. An entire area of research is aimed at trying to identify the factors that determine who will express their "addiction genes" and who won't. Making these kinds of predictions, unfortunately, is an inexact science at this point, and there is a long way to go before doctors will be able to do it reliably.

Environmental factors

Environmental factors, such as one's daily social interactions, play a large role in the development of addiction. Let's start with some influences that should be obvious to most of us— factors that influence the choices of a person who is already addicted or well on the road to addiction. For example, living in close proximity to family members or friends struggling with addiction makes it more difficult for someone with genetic predisposition to addiction to stay away from drugs. Again, this predicament made things more difficult for Jason in our case study. Similarly, if a person is in recovery—having established a drug-free lifestyle—being around those who are using drugs or alcohol regularly is risky. These situations contain cues, or signals, in the form of behaviors or objects that trigger a craving or desire to use drugs. Those with a history of addiction have a high level of sensitivity to these signals (called "cue reactivity"). A person with a history of alcoholism, for example, will react far more strongly to seeing someone drink alcohol than someone without such a history. Due to this high level of cue reactivity and the likelihood that such cues can trigger a relapse, many types of talk therapy treatments for addiction try to modify the addicted person's response to cues via learning and memory.[28] Patients learn alternative ways to respond to potentially triggering cues and then, when confronted with these cues again, remember that these cues do not necessarily mean they will relapse to their drug-using behavior.

But environmental factors do not need to directly involve alcohol or other drugs to affect someone's ability to steer clear of addiction. Other psychosocial stressors—stressful situations revolving around important social categories like work or relationships (finding out that your girlfriend is unexpectedly pregnant, like Jason did, for example)—can lead someone to begin using mood-altering substances or, if they already have a history of addiction, relapse. This is why treatment professionals often recommend a period of time away from work if someone has just completed an addiction treatment program. While abstinence from alcohol and other drugs is typically established during a structured treatment program, rushing right back into one's life and the stressors that likely played an important role in the person's need to enter the program is a risky idea.

Physiological factors

Physiological factors play a large role in addiction. This is not a surprise, given that many people describe addiction as a "brain disease." Addiction causes your brain to undergo changes at its most basic levels—within the cells, which are the building blocks of your body's organs, including the brain. These changes occur immediately (also called "acutely") in response to a cue, a stressor, or drug use itself. They also occur after an extended period of use (also called "chronically"). Here's how that works.

Drug use leads to the release of brain chemicals called "neurotransmitters." One of these chemicals, dopamine, is released in an area of the brain called the "nucleus accumbens," or pleasure center. Research shows that dopamine levels in the brain surge after someone engages in a pleasurable activity, such as having sex, eating, drinking alcohol, and using other drugs, including marijuana. Your body associates the activity with the good feelings of a dopamine surge and, consequently, you want to repeat the activity to experience that pleasurable sensation again. These surges help to explain why some people smoke marijuana every day even though it harms other areas of their lives.

Using drugs like marijuana causes immediate changes to brain cells as well as changes that take place over time with chronic use. When a person uses drugs, the drugs enter the body and are then broken down into chemicals that bind to special receptors throughout the body. The chemicals are the "keys" plugging into the receptors, which are the "locks." When people use drugs over and over, this process occurs again and again, and after a while, the receptors get worn out and the body cannot produce enough new receptors to replace the worn-out ones. The result is what is called "down-regulation," the decreased production of the particular receptors associated with the drug being used.

A reduction in the number of receptors is one factor in the development of tolerance. Tolerance means that a substance user must use an increasing amount, or dose, of a drug in order to achieve the same effects that they once got from a lower dose of the drug. When the receptor numbers are reduced, the user tries to compensate by using more drugs. Those with addiction commonly describe this predicament, where they need to use more and more of the drug to get the same effect. Getting more and more of the drug usually leads to an entirely new set of problems, such as how to find and afford the larger amount.

Other physiological factors play a role in addiction as well. Jason experienced unpleasant withdrawal symptoms, such as insomnia, when he tried to stop using marijuana, and these symptoms made it harder for him to maintain abstinence from marijuana (we will discuss marijuana withdrawal in more detail in chapter 5).

There is a growing body of research looking at the differences between men and women and how they relate to addiction. For example, compared to men, women may begin using lower doses of drugs, their use may progress more rapidly into addiction, and they may be more likely to relapse once initial abstinence is established.[29] These differences also must be considered in treatment—different types of talk therapies or medications may be more helpful for men than women, or vice versa.

Other medical conditions or psychiatric illnesses can play an important role in the addiction process. Depression is a classic example. People suffering from depression may look to alcohol or other drugs to escape their low mood and other symptoms of depression that bother them. The use of drugs in these cases may only lead to temporary relief from their problems or uncomfortable feelings. Ultimately, use of mood-altering substances often exacerbates feelings of depression, especially when the feelings of being intoxicated subside.

As noted earlier, anxiety is another example that is particularly relevant to marijuana use. Many people who use marijuana say they use it to treat anxiety. While we explained in chapter 3 how regular marijuana use actually leads to worsening anxiety over the long term, clearly many people would not use marijuana nearly as frequently as they do if they were not bothered by symptoms of anxiety. This is why, when someone seeks treatment for either anxiety or problems with marijuana use, the clinician needs to ask about the other in the clinical interview. It is important to understand why someone would use marijuana, and it is also important to understand what someone's anxiety may revolve around. When you consider the strong relationship between anxiety and marijuana, it is easy to appreciate how the effective treatment of anxiety, either with talk therapy or medications, can affect someone's marijuana use.

Summary

In this chapter, you've learned that marijuana truly is addictive. Addiction is the repeated use of a substance despite harm, and it results from a combination of historical, environmental, and physiological factors. Addiction affects multiple areas of a person's life: work, school, and relationships. By the time patients end up sitting across from me in my office, they usually have had problems in these important areas of their lives. They talk of the wreckage of addiction—blown opportunities and fractured relationships. When a patient is having a conversation with me during the initial evaluation, it is often difficult to tell the difference between someone addicted to marijuana and someone addicted to "hard drugs" like heroin or cocaine. That is because, as with heroin and cocaine addicts, people addicted to marijuana have a brain disease and are engaging in compulsive behaviors that hurt themselves and those around them. Marijuana, as the drug of addiction in this case, hijacks the normal circuits in the brain first and then, eventually, negatively affects the person's motivation and ability to prioritize.

5

MYTH #3

Stopping Use of Marijuana Does Not Cause Withdrawal

In this chapter, we will be exploring exactly what it is about marijuana's potential addictiveness that makes it so hard for people to stop using, even when they might be very motivated to do so.

Kristen

Kristen had been smoking marijuana for years. She started smoking marijuana every day about three years ago, initially just as a relaxing way to unwind after a long day as a cashier at an electronics store. She loved to watch *The Office* on her laptop, and the best way to do that, she felt, was to sit out on her porch and watch it while smoking marijuana. After a few months, she found herself smoking on days she wasn't working, also to relax. A few more months slipped by and Kristen was smoking in the mornings before work; she wasn't excited about her job and thought that smoking before work made the day at the store more tolerable.

She settled into this pattern for more than a year and realized around the beginning of the new year that she was frustrated with her life and, especially, her career. She had worked hard during college and made sacrifices to do as well as she could. She did not do these things to end up in this position and, in examining her life, she thought two things about her marijuana use: (1) it might be holding her back in her career, and (2) no matter where she saw herself in five years, she did not picture herself smoking daily as she was now.

So she tried to stop smoking, just like that. Unfortunately, it was much harder than she had thought it would be—she felt irritable and anxious, and she had trouble sleeping as she avoided smoking for almost two days. She was frustrated; her friends always said that marijuana was not addictive, so why was this so hard? On the second night, as she tossed and turned, unable to get to sleep, she said "Forget it" and packed a bowl of marijuana.

The Experience of Withdrawal

When people who are smoking marijuana daily or nearly every day try to stop smoking, they experience withdrawal symptoms. These include the symptoms that Kristen experienced—anxiety, irritability, and difficulty sleeping—but we'll talk more about these a little later on. Withdrawal is different from the other two marijuana myths we've discussed thus far. While some people debate whether marijuana is harmful or whether marijuana is addictive, withdrawal does not seem to be on the radar. Most people have not even thought about whether stopping marijuana use causes withdrawal symptoms.

For years the scientific literature has described a marijuana withdrawal syndrome. The evidence for this syndrome has grown to such a degree that the American Psychiatric Association added marijuana withdrawal syndrome to the most recent edition of its guidebook of psychiatric classification, *DSM-5*. Alan Budney and Ryan Vandrey, two prominent substance abuse researchers from Dartmouth and Johns Hopkins, respectively, have conducted a series of studies that have demonstrated that marijuana withdrawal symptoms are very similar to nicotine withdrawal symptoms.[30] These symptoms make up the marijuana withdrawal syndrome described in *DSM-5*. The syndrome occurs after someone stops using marijuana after having used it heavily for an extended period of time. Budney and Vandrey showed that although both marijuana withdrawal and nicotine withdrawal have many of the same symptoms—irritability, anxiety, and difficulty sleeping, to name a few—the degrees to which people experience withdrawal from either substance varies somewhat. Overall, though, the experiences are very similar: people feel lousy and these feelings often result in continued use of marijuana or tobacco.

"Using heavily" means smoking a lot of marijuana daily or nearly every day. We have defined regular use as at least four times per week, but practically, regular users typically use six or seven days a week. To take it a step further, most users who smoke daily or nearly every day smoke multiple times a day. There are not many people who smoke once a day and use a small amount when they smoke. Most people who use marijuana either use rarely or regularly, with just a few in the middle. People either really like marijuana and use it very often, or they are indifferent to it and therefore may or may not smoke marijuana when it is offered to them. This is different from alcohol, where the distribution of use is spread out fairly evenly, from rarely to daily to just about everything in between. This pattern of using marijuana—either using a lot or using very rarely (if at all)—may be influenced by the illegal status of marijuana in most of the United States that limits its availability. People have to really want to use it to use it regularly—although that may be changing if the trend toward legalization continues.

Marijuana withdrawal symptoms begin within a few days of stopping heavy marijuana use. Besides those listed above, symptoms can also include anger, feelings of aggression, depressed mood, and loss of appetite. Physical symptoms of withdrawal may include headaches, stomach pains, increased sweating, fever, chills, or shakiness. These withdrawal symptoms are severe enough to interfere with the person's functioning at work or in social situations. To be classified as withdrawal, these symptoms cannot be explained by the presence of other physical or mental health problems.

Most of us know people who have tried to stop using addictive substances. Many of us are familiar with how difficult it can be to stop smoking cigarettes and, more recently, we have learned how difficult it is to stop using opioids like oxycodone or heroin. Thinking of marijuana withdrawal as being similar to nicotine withdrawal is helpful. If you have tried to stop smoking cigarettes before (or know someone who has), you know that when people quit smoking, nicotine withdrawal makes them extremely irritable and anxious. During withdrawal, they don't want to be around other people, and most people don't want to be around *them* for fear of receiving their wrath. When trying to quit, it is very difficult to concentrate and it is also a challenge to be engaged in family or social activities. Those trying to quit nicotine are constantly fighting the urge to give in and smoke. Quitting marijuana is the same way; this is another example of how marijuana is similar to drugs that we recognize as addictive and difficult to quit.

One advantage of the lack of public awareness of the marijuana withdrawal syndrome, however, is that clinicians can use this as a powerful clinical tool. I talk about withdrawal in every initial evaluation of patients with possible marijuana problems, and many of these patients are relieved when they learn about marijuana withdrawal syndrome. These withdrawal symptoms—feeling absolutely miserable—often lead to relapse to marijuana use, just as nicotine withdrawal can lead to a relapse to cigarette use or opioid withdrawal (feeling "dope sick") can lead to a relapse to the use of oxycodone, heroin, or other opium-related drug. This occurred in the case study presented at the beginning of the chapter. Kristen attempted to stop using marijuana and was fully committed to doing so until she experienced withdrawal.

Part of what makes stopping marijuana use so difficult is that people do not expect to experience withdrawal symptoms. Kristen was not expecting these symptoms, so it came as a surprise to her that she was not feeling well physically, and this development may have led her to feel pessimistic about her chances of quitting. This pessimism—feeling that there is no way to succeed at quitting—often makes it easier for someone to give in and relapse. It is easier to deal with a challenging situation that you are expecting than with a problem that comes as a complete surprise.

In talking with patients with marijuana addiction who have had multiple failed attempts to quit, this is a common theme. They were not aware of the physical withdrawal symptoms they would experience and were ill-prepared to deal with feeling irritable, anxious, and physically sick. Patients who may be addicted to marijuana and have yet to quit may not realize that they have already experienced withdrawal symptoms; they are not aware of the symptoms because they aren't looking for them. Only in talking with them about their experiences with trying to quit does it become apparent that they were having marijuana withdrawal symptoms and these symptoms were hindering their attempts.

Patients often describe a sense of relief when they learn about the marijuana withdrawal syndrome, as it validates their difficulties in stopping their use of marijuana. The withdrawal syndrome provides a conceptual framework that can help them understand why they have found it so difficult to stop using a drug that their friends say is not addictive. This is an example of how educating a patient about the science of marijuana can be a great way to jump-start treatment. Covering this topic in the first hour of an initial evaluation often provides patients with important knowledge they did not have before they sought treatment. This new knowledge prepares them for what may lie ahead if they try to quit, and being prepared may help them succeed where they'd previously faltered.

Summary

Most people do not believe that marijuana use can cause withdrawal. In fact, most people have never thought about withdrawal and marijuana use together. However, marijuana withdrawal, for those who have used marijuana regularly for extended periods of time, is very real. Marijuana withdrawal syndrome is associated with anxiety, irritability, difficulty sleeping, and other troublesome symptoms. It is like nicotine withdrawal in many ways, and having withdrawal symptoms when you are trying to quit makes it much harder to actually quit. In our case study, Kristen had every intention of quitting, but she was not expecting to battle withdrawal symptoms, so her first attempts to quit were unsuccessful. When patients learn about marijuana withdrawal syndrome, they often are relieved because the withdrawal syndrome provides at least a partial explanation for why they have struggled to stop using a drug that they often have heard is harmless and not addictive.

SECTION III

POLICY

6

Decriminalization and Legalization of Recreational Marijuana

Decriminalization of marijuana and legalization of marijuana have become popular topics of conversation in recent years. Along with the issue of medical marijuana, the United States faces two key legal issues in regard to the drug: decriminalization and legalization of recreational use. Although marijuana remains an illegal drug on a federal level, as of November 2014, seventeen states have decriminalized marijuana and four states— Washington, Colorado, Alaska, and Oregon—have voted to legalize the recreational use of marijuana.

States typically phase in these changes, first by decriminalizing marijuana, then by legalizing certain medical uses of marijuana, and finally, by possibly legalizing its recreational use. Decriminalization and legalization are issues that share several key elements, so it is useful to look at these two issues in the same chapter.

This chapter aims to explain the concepts of decriminalization of marijuana and the legalization of the recreational use of marijuana and to provide a balanced overview of the arguments for and against both decriminalization and legalization. There are very few places where one can examine the key arguments on these issues presented with limited bias. Finally, I will discuss my perspective on these difficult policy issues.

Decriminalization

Decriminalization of marijuana possession laws refers to steps taken to remove the criminal penalties associated with possessing small amounts of marijuana. Decriminalization laws make the possession of small amounts of marijuana a civil rather than criminal infraction. "Small amounts" are what one person would typically use during a short period of time ("personal use"). It is important to note that under decriminalization laws, possession of marijuana is *not* legal. Possession is still illegal, but the penalty can be a civil or criminal penalty depending on the amount of marijuana in the person's possession. Decriminalization laws attempt to treat small amounts of marijuana like alcohol: Public use and possession is frowned upon and can result in a penalty, just as drinking alcohol in public places can result in an "open container" infraction. I will state this for emphasis, however: *decriminalization is not the same as legalization.*

So, what does this mean in practice? When marijuana possession is decriminalized, law enforcement officials who find people in possession of an amount of marijuana under certain stipulated quantities—usually an ounce—can give these individuals a civil infraction ticket. This ticket usually entails a small fine. In some states that have decriminalized marijuana possession, law enforcement officials have the option to mandate substance abuse education for the offender. But, if the offense isn't considered criminal, the offender cannot be sent to prison. Interestingly, in some states, these civil infractions become criminal if they occur enough times. In New York State, for example, the first two times you are caught possessing small amounts of marijuana, you receive a violation and a fine. These violations still may cause problems beyond the fine; for instance, such a violation may affect the person's ability to obtain student financial aid. The third time someone is caught in New York State with a small amount of marijuana, however, that person may receive a criminal misdemeanor charge. (A "misdemeanor" is a crime that is considered to be of low seriousness.)

Legalization

Legalizing the recreational use of marijuana is the next logical step after decriminalizing the possession of small amounts of marijuana. While twenty-three states and the District of Columbia have passed medical marijuana laws, usually following decriminalization, legalization is more directly associated with decriminalization. Decriminalization and legalization exist along a continuum, with decriminalization representing the first step in softening the stance toward marijuana possession and use, and legalization representing the end of this spectrum. While, under decriminalization laws, adults found in possession of small amounts of marijuana would still receive a civil penalty, legalizing the drug removes any penalty—civil or criminal—for possessing a certain amount of marijuana by those twenty-one years of age and older. Legalization is the antithesis of prohibition, so legalization affects many other aspects of marijuana. If legalized, marijuana would be treated as a commodity; this would mean legal production, distribution, and sale in addition to the legal possession and use that first comes to mind. Legalization has been pushed forward by marijuana advocates; in November 2013, Washington and Colorado voted to treat marijuana like alcohol, restricting legal possession to residents age twenty-one and older.

When the issue of legalization of marijuana comes up, comparisons to alcohol and, to a lesser degree, nicotine inevitably arise. The history of alcohol in the United States is a useful case study when considering legalization of marijuana. Prohibition of alcohol centered on the manufacture, transport, and sale of alcohol. Prohibition of alcohol began in the United States in 1920 with the passage of the Eighteenth Amendment. Alcohol had long been a part of American life when religious groups and health advocates took aim at drinking for both moral and health reasons. The temperance movement began pushing against drinking in the 1840s, and momentum continued to build until the passage of the Eighteenth Amendment. Prohibition of alcohol was considered largely unsuccessful, as Americans continued to drink in large numbers. Eventually, a political movement against Prohibition ensued; this movement pointed to the hypocritical nature of the law given that so many Americans continued to drink, as well as the potential tax revenue that could be generated from legal alcohol production and sale. The Twenty-First Amendment repealed Prohibition in 1933. Today, both alcohol and tobacco are legal and heavily taxed. Unfortunately, large numbers of Americans continue to use both alcohol and nicotine to excess, resulting in tremendous health and societal costs.

Decriminalizing marijuana or legalization of the recreational use of marijuana may occur in a complex set of circumstances, as explored in the first five chapters of this book. These circumstances include social and cultural conditions as well as pharmacological facts. We have a long and confused history regarding the drug, and we labor under a number of myths that polarize opinions about it. The net result is that we, as a society, don't know how to relate to this drug responsibly. We can't decide if it is a threat to the public and individual good that must be severely constrained, a potential benefit, or a matter of personal liberty. This is not unlike our relationship to two other potentially addictive drugs that threaten health and can damage society: alcohol and nicotine. Keep in mind as we explore the pros and cons of decriminalization of marijuana and legalization of marijuana that even with these other two popular drugs, we have a mixed and confused history of use, misuse, social benefit, and social damage. We're still working out the "right" solution for alcohol and tobacco. Thus, we should get used to the idea that the "right" solution for marijuana may change over time. This has even happened in the Netherlands. Their lax drug policies have been held up by many legalization proponents as a case for making recreational marijuana legal. While marijuana is still technically illegal there, small amounts of marijuana are available for purchase in coffee shops. However, buyers now need to have proof of residency (although enforcement of this recent law is said to be lax). Further, you must be eighteen or older to purchase it and can't buy more than five grams per day. Legislation has also been proposed that would add marijuana with more than 15 percent THC to their illegal "hard" drugs list, which would prohibit its sale to the public.

Both decriminalization of marijuana and the legalization of the recreational use of marijuana are complex issues. (Legalization of medical marijuana, which we will discuss in chapter 7, is more straightforward, particularly if the scope of medical marijuana laws are limited as discussed in that chapter.) Recall from chapter 1 that the United States already has a convoluted history with marijuana; it was legal for a period until 1937. Just as this book describes both the potential benefits and the potential dangers of marijuana in as balanced a fashion as possible, it discusses the merits of arguments in support of decriminalization of marijuana and legalization of marijuana and those opposed to these same moves. I aim to discuss both sides of the issue so that readers can consider both with improved objectivity. Therefore, I'll start by reviewing in detail the rationale offered by those who believe that marijuana should be decriminalized or legalized.

Arguments in Favor of
Decriminalization and Legalization

The first argument in favor of legalizing marijuana is that legalization would increase personal liberties of U.S. citizens. Those in favor of legalization feel that the government infringes on the personal rights and freedoms of Americans with its current marijuana laws and that the government has no right to enforce laws related to the use of marijuana. At the Virginia Convention of 1775, Patrick Henry, one of the United States' founding fathers, said, "Give me liberty or give me death." While this famous statement concerned whether or not the American colonies should break away from English rule, these words remain an important part of our country's values today. We believe in the freedom to make important choices in America. Some of these choices are beneficial to us, and some are harmful to us—but the ability to make these choices is considered a fundamental American right. When the government passes laws that infringe upon these rights, it draws the ire of people who hold firmly to the right to make such choices. In general, Republicans and Libertarians are the political groups that make the most noise when the right to make decisions is infringed upon by the government. There are many products that we are free to buy and consume that have the potential to cause us great harm. Therefore, just because people may be harmed as a result of decriminalization of marijuana or legalization of marijuana does not mean that these policies should be avoided. Obviously, people make foolish choices every day in a variety of areas not limited to substance use, but part of being American is having the right to make those choices, whether they are good or bad choices.

Those in favor of legalization of the recreational use of marijuana make a strong economic argument as well. Both alcohol and tobacco have been subject to excise taxes in the United

States. "Excise taxes" are additional taxes for specific items—alcohol and tobacco in this case—paid on top of sales taxes. Excise taxes are indirect taxes, meaning that the seller who pays the tax to the government is supposed to recover the tax revenue by raising the price of the item. States have raised significant amounts of revenue this way, some of it earmarked for specific programs, even substance abuse treatment in some cases. Excise taxes also serve the purpose of making alcohol and tobacco more expensive to purchase. As the price goes up, people purchase less of the (potentially harmful) product. That means they consume less, which reduces the risk associated with the product. The role of higher tobacco costs due to increased taxes in the decrease in the number of smokers over the past several years is an example. The argument for legalization is that the government could then apply excise taxes, collecting revenues, some of which could be used to fund programs that reduced the harms associated with marijuana. These taxes would also necessitate pricing marijuana high enough to (in theory) keep its use minimal, but not so high as to induce a new black market—just as is done with alcohol and tobacco.

In addition to excise taxes, experts have described other ways in which legalization of the recreational use of marijuana would be a smart financial move. Harvard economist Jeffrey Miron, in his report "The Budgetary Implications of Marijuana Prohibition," argued how marijuana legalization, by replacing marijuana prohibition with a system of taxation and regulation, has the potential to save the United States $7.7 billion per year in state and federal funds that are currently spent to enforce prohibition.[31] Miron also wrote that legalization of marijuana would result in at least $2.4 billion in tax revenues annually if marijuana were taxed in the same manner as most consumer goods. If we taxed marijuana in the same way we tax alcohol or tobacco—with an excise tax—we could raise as much as $6.2

billion annually. Numbers like these get lots of attention, which is part of the reason that legalization of the recreational use of marijuana is being so hotly debated across the United States.

Another advantage of decriminalization and legalization is that these policies decrease the need for a black market of marijuana sales. While both sides of the debate argue about whether or not there will be a black market if marijuana is legalized, it seems likely that there still will be, but probably to a lesser degree than that which currently exists. This black market will sell to anyone, including children, while avoiding taxation; these are reasons to attempt to limit it. The black market also does not take responsibility for the problems it causes, so cutting into the black market in favor of a legitimate sales avenue should reduce several of the current problems related to marijuana sales.

Another argument in favor of decriminalization and legalization concerns the difficulty and cost of enforcing criminal penalties. The issue of how to enforce marijuana laws isn't an easy one. Undoubtedly, it is both expensive and difficult to enforce laws related to use of a substance that close to nineteen million Americans used last month. Even if you are strongly opposed to the idea of recreational marijuana use, you must still wonder how much time and money should be spent by law enforcement officers to enforce laws related to marijuana when there are other problems, perhaps more serious problems, that require the attention of these officers. Each time we read about crimes that are not investigated properly, we must question whether law enforcement agencies have adequate resources to investigate these crimes and, if so, whether they are using them effectively. Not necessarily the next question to ask, but certainly one that should be asked if thinking about these instances in depth, is how these situations might be changed if the recreational use of marijuana was legal. As with many complex issues, there are no easy answers here.

A related argument in favor of decriminalizing marijuana and legalizing recreational use is that it will reduce incarceration rates related to marijuana and its costs. With the current set of laws and criminal penalties (where they are still applicable), many feel that these punishments do not fit the "crime" of possessing small amounts of marijuana for personal use. It is important to draw a distinction here between the possession of small amounts of marijuana that you plan to use yourself and the possession of larger amounts that you intend to sell to others, usually as a way to make a profit. Legalization would move the sale of marijuana from neighborhood drug dealers to private vendors. While this might not completely eliminate the "black market," it should greatly reduce it. There will likely still be individuals who see an opportunity to make money either by selling different strains than those offered by stores or by selling marijuana at a price lower than what stores might offer. For example, black market marijuana sales have continued in Washington and Colorado despite recent legalization there. Nevertheless, the creation of stores that sell marijuana like they sell alcohol and tobacco—by properly registering with state government—should significantly reduce black market sales. These stores would offer a layer of regulation that should benefit both individuals and states. The creation of regulated stores· should make marijuana safer by controlling its composition and it should, as discussed above, bring tax revenues to the state. Effective decriminalization laws should be enough to handle the issue of punishment, although we will discuss below how the amount of marijuana allowed under the decriminalization laws is higher than it should be. That is, lowering the amount to one-fourth of an ounce would do a better job matching the spirit of the law, to minimize penalties for possessing marijuana for personal use while continuing to appropriately punish those who intend to function as drug dealers and distribute marijuana to others. This issue is still alive in most states, though, as only seventeen states have decriminalized the marijuana laws as of this writing.

Decriminalization of marijuana and legalization of the recreational use of marijuana would rid society of current marijuana laws, which appear to discriminate against minorities. This is yet another emotionally charged issue in the marijuana debate, and people on both sides make compelling cases. Organizations such as the Marijuana Policy Project and the National Organization for the Reform of Marijuana Laws (NORML) and some experts in the field of substance abuse research, like Dr. Carl Hart from Columbia University, state unequivocally that the current laws are racially biased. An example of this is the data from the District of Columbia, where African Americans are eight times more likely to get arrested for possession of marijuana than their white counterparts. In 2007, 12.2 percent of African Americans in DC (about one of every eight) used marijuana, as did 10.5 percent of whites (about one of every nine). These percentages are quite close, and one would expect that the percentages of African American and white people arrested for marijuana would be about the same. But 91 percent—nine out of ten—marijuana possession arrests were of African Americans, while only 8 percent of these arrests were of white people.[32] It is hard to ignore this data, especially when such arrests may be an entry point into the criminal justice system. These arrests can have major implications for the offender, especially when added to other criminal charges. Marijuana advocates point to the family courts, where women can lose custody of their children as a result of marijuana possession charges, depending on other factors in their cases. And while a marijuana possession charge alone for a first-time offender, for example, will not lead to incarceration or the loss of child custody, a legitimate question is whether such charges should ever do so. If we agree that the use of small amounts of marijuana should be treated like the use of alcohol, then the answer to this question is "no."

In states without marijuana decriminalization laws, possession of these small amounts of marijuana remains a criminal offense that results in a fine and a court date. In addition, these criminal charges may be considered in the context of other criminal charges, resulting in additional criminal penalties. Therefore, the possession charge itself may not bring about significant punishment, but the charge may trigger very serious penalties, including jail, when considered alongside other criminal charges the offender may have already had. These may be instances where the punishment does not fit the crime.

Another reason for decriminalization and legalization is that the majority of Americans are in favor of these policies. While the majority of the population does not always make the right choice (we have explored reasons for this starting in chapter 3 when we introduced the myths that underline why there is a gap between the scientific truth about marijuana and the public perception), it is important to note public sentiment when considering these important policy issues. During alcohol Prohibition, the majority of Americans did not believe in the concepts behind the laws, and the idea failed in part due to this lack of buy-in. This same idea should be applied to marijuana. However, I encourage everyone to try to become as educated as possible about the issue before they formulate their stance. No policy on this controversial issue will be perfect, but this may be an instance where a deal is cut with a well-crafted policy designed to mitigate the risks of decriminalization and legalization.

Finally, decriminalization and legalization of marijuana may ultimately result in less use of other harmful drugs. It is too early to know if this will be the case, but it is a possibility that increased use of marijuana may result in less use of alcohol, opioids, or other harmful drugs. A recent paper documented a relationship between states with medical marijuana laws and fewer deaths from opioid overdoses in comparison to states without medical marijuana laws.[33] This argument is bolstered if one makes the case that marijuana is less harmful than alcohol or opioids; this would be a harm reduction method of sorts. This is yet another issue that we will continue to monitor in states that have legalized the recreational use of marijuana.

Arguments against Decriminalization and Legalization

Now let's explore some of the potential negative consequences of decriminalizing marijuana possession and legalizing recreational marijuana. Keep in mind, these are arguments designed to reflect the challenges of implementing these policies today, with an understanding that the data is always changing, so the best solutions may change as well.

The first argument against the decriminalization and legalization of marijuana is that these policies would lead to increased access and use of marijuana, thereby leading to increased problems associated with marijuana use, especially addiction. This leads to perhaps the only point that both pro- and anti-marijuana advocates agree upon—*no one wants to see increased access to marijuana for young people.*

As we saw in chapter 3, marijuana is potentially addictive and regular use while a young person's brain is still developing can have many adverse consequences, including a decline in brain function as measured by IQ. In chapter 2, we learned that about 9 percent of adults who use marijuana and about 17 percent of young people who use marijuana become addicted. Therefore, it is unquestionably a concern that policies that promote easier access to marijuana might lead to increased use among all groups and, therefore, increased adverse consequences. Consequences such as health problems, addiction, and decreased work productivity all result in financial costs. Data from states with medical marijuana laws shows greater increases in marijuana use compared to states without medical marijuana laws during the same time periods. Importantly, we must note that it is too early to draw conclusions from data from Colorado and Washington State, the first two states to legalize recreational marijuana.

The related argument against decriminalization and legalization of the recreational use of marijuana is whether we want to repeat our history with alcohol and nicotine. As mentioned above, those in favor of legalization tout the potential tax revenue that would come from legalization. But note that legalizing tobacco and alcohol has contributed to significant societal problems and costs as well. For example, tobacco use is the number one preventable cause of death in the United States, contributing to more than 480,000 deaths annually.[34] How do we begin to think about that number? Well, consider that on average a large jet carries 400 people. Now imagine if in the United States 1,000 such jets crashed *each year.* Would you fly? Wouldn't you be outraged and demand that something be done? That's what we tolerate with legal nicotine. The numbers for alcohol are considerable as well, with alcohol thought to contribute to at least 100,000 deaths each year.

The degree to which use would escalate is unclear, but we should recognize that the use rates might increase significantly when companies that sell tobacco and alcohol enter the market. The tobacco and alcohol companies are highly successful businesses that are very skilled at marketing and sales. They would quickly transfer those skills to the marketing and sales of marijuana. It is worth pointing out, of course, that some of the advertising and marketing tactics employed by the tobacco companies have been called deceptive and unethical. One example of this was the famous "Joe Camel" ads that were determined to be aimed at minors; these ads were subsequently pulled from the market after public outrage. Of course, the advertising that these companies are allowed to do could be regulated by law. However, alcohol and tobacco companies have had their advertising regulated to some degree already and they still have, at different times, targeted specific groups with their ads, including young people. The idea of having the alcohol and tobacco companies involved in the marketing of another potentially harmful and addictive substance is chilling, and this is another reason that we must carefully think through the issue of legalization before we move forward with it in any additional states.

Many people oppose decriminalization and legalization of marijuana for moral reasons. These people feel strongly that all drug use is wrong, and they have a particular difficulty in understanding why the government would allow its citizens to participate in a morally corrupt behavior. Religious views may play a role here, with fundamentalists being more likely to oppose policies that make it easier to get marijuana, but there are people who feel that taking mind-altering drugs is just the wrong thing to do and, by extension, laws and policies that promote (or at least don't restrict) these ideas are morally wrong as well. The morality argument is tied into a couple of other arguments against decriminalization and legalization, both having to do with how these policies endorse a questionable behavior. The first is that these policies send the message that society approves of a type of drug use and that society should not promote the use of drugs or the seeking of mind-altering experiences. The second is that, by enacting these policies, individual states are condoning potentially harmful behavior. Granted, that has not stopped states from promoting alcohol use, tobacco use, or gambling in some ways, but it is important to note that there are significant numbers of people who do not believe the government should be involved in such activities.

Another argument against decriminalization and legalization of marijuana is that these policies may remove any deterrent effect that the criminal charges had; people who were concerned about being arrested for marijuana possession might be less concerned about being caught with marijuana, especially if they are in possession of an amount less than the limit stipulated by the law. When talking about decriminalization during my educational seminars, I like to use a clinical experience of mine as an example of what these laws can mean. Massachusetts decriminalized possession of less than one ounce of marijuana in 2008. A patient I was working with at the time, for a psychiatric issue not related to addiction of any sort, worked in the cafeteria at a local university. He told me that while at work at the cafeteria, cigarette breaks had become marijuana breaks because any worries of being hassled about getting caught with marijuana in public were now gone. This is just one instance, but it does raise the possibility that these laws can remove any reservations people have about using marijuana in public.

Decriminalization laws may remove the "teeth" that come with a criminal charge in the eyes of law enforcement officials. Law enforcement officials are often part of understaffed, overworked departments, and they might not investigate possible possession situations with as much zeal as they did previously, knowing that the result would be a civil infraction only. These law enforcement officials might not be blamed for thinking they have "bigger fish to fry" than civil violations such as this. We discussed previously how this might also be a reason to decriminalize marijuana, in that it would free up understaffed police departments to address more serious crimes.

Another drawback to decriminalization and legalization is that these policies tacitly endorse a black market. While both sides of the debate argue about whether or not there will be a black market if marijuana is legalized, it seems likely that there *will* be a black market and that it will sell to anyone, including children.

An important question: Driving under the influence

The probable increase in marijuana-impaired driving is a major argument against legalization that raises complex questions worth exploring in more depth. Research on the effects of marijuana on driving is still under way. A recent study demonstrated that more young people are driving after using marijuana themselves or riding as passengers in cars driven by those who have recently used.[35] We do know that the degree of impairment depends on a variety of factors, including the amount smoked and its potency, the time of use in relation to driving, and the user's level of experience with marijuana. Marijuana can cause impairment in every performance area associated with the operation of a vehicle, including motor coordination, visual tracking of objects, attentiveness, perception of time and speed, and the use of new information. While it is helpful to think of impairment of driving related to marijuana use as similar to the impairment seen after drinking alcohol, there are differences in the effects produced by marijuana use and the effects produced by alcohol use. Decriminalization and legalization of marijuana may make our roads less safe by increasing the number of drivers operating motor vehicles under the influence of marijuana.

It would be great if we could apply the same rules we have for driving under the influence of alcohol to driving under the influence of marijuana. Unfortunately, measuring the degree of impairment caused by marijuana is not a matter of administering a simple Breathalyzer test or of asking how much one has consumed.

One important difference between marijuana use and alcohol use is that it is more difficult to carefully control the dosage of marijuana consumed. Even the strongest alcohol usually requires at least two "shots" in order to start to feel the effects. It is rare to feel impaired after one standard alcoholic drink. Marijuana is usually dosed in "hits" or inhalations from a bong, blunt, joint, or other form, and it is not uncommon for someone to feel impaired after one hit. In fact, a typical smoking session may feature only two hits of marijuana at a time. This is relevant when thinking about more potent forms of marijuana. While someone may smoke less high-potency marijuana to get a desired effect, it is more difficult for less experienced users or users who weigh less to control the effects of strong marijuana that they may smoke.

Another important difference between driving while impaired by alcohol and while impaired by marijuana is the nature of the effects. Driving studies conducted with people under the influence of marijuana have shown only modest impairments. Data suggests that experienced marijuana smokers in particular show little functional impairment when driving. Some researchers have suggested that unlike drivers under the influence of alcohol, who often underestimate their level of impairment, drivers under the influence of marijuana may overestimate their level of impairment and then compensate accordingly.[36] Research shows that marijuana-impaired drivers have difficulty staying in the correct lane. However, perhaps because they are aware of that difficulty, they drive slower, pass other drivers less frequently, and maintain a greater following distance behind other cars than those driving under the influence of alcohol. These compensatory mechanisms cannot defend against all types of impairment, though. People impaired by marijuana have decreased reaction times and are more likely to respond incorrectly to emergency situations.

It's important to note that more research needs to be done in the area of marijuana's impact on driving, since it will likely become a more critical issue as the number of possible applications for marijuana—medical or recreational—increases.

Overall, it appears that marijuana impairs one's ability to drive, but perhaps not to the same degree that alcohol does due to the tendency for marijuana-impaired drivers to employ compensatory mechanisms. A related problem is that people may also drive under the *combined* influence of marijuana and alcohol. Here, the research is clear: the combination of marijuana and alcohol is dangerous, resulting in far worse outcomes than those produced from driving under the influence of either drug alone.

Currently we don't have the equivalent of a Breathalyzer test for marijuana, nor do we have a measurement of how much marijuana creates impairment. Marijuana and alcohol are metabolized, or processed, by the body in different ways. Therefore, it is not possible to do a Breathalyzer for marijuana use. But we should be able to do the research to compare the effects of alcohol and marijuana on driving and construct a comparative curve showing levels of alcohol and marijuana along with their relative levels of impairment. This would allow us to know what level of marijuana use is roughly equivalent to the impairment caused by alcohol at the .08 blood alcohol content (the current legal limit for driving under the influence of alcohol).

So, one problem is that we lack a good dose-response curve for marijuana that would allow us to determine how much creates impairment. But even if we *did* have that information, we currently lack the technology to allow our law enforcement to test for marijuana impairment effectively in the field. Colorado has made do thus far by drawing blood to determine impairment from marijuana use, but this method is much less practical than a Breathalyzer used for alcohol. Many in Colorado and other states recognize that having field-ready technology akin to a Breathalyzer is essential and are working feverishly to develop such a tool.

To be clear, one can be convicted now of driving under the influence of marijuana using a test of coordination and, in some instances, blood levels. But a test of coordination alone does not produce the sensitivity needed for fair law enforcement. If someone is unable to stand as a result of marijuana use or are otherwise grossly impaired, that person may be convicted. But it is the subtler levels of impairment that would be important to catch as well, and a test of coordination alone cannot do this.

Colorado, for one, has added a blood test as a second method of determining impairment. While a combination of coordination tests and blood tests is better than either alone, the blood test is not ideal. But a blood test for marijuana is less effective than a blood test for alcohol (or a Breathalyzer, for that matter) for several reasons. First, marijuana is processed much more slowly by the body than alcohol, which is processed at a relatively fast and predictable rate. So an individual could smoke lots of marijuana on a Monday and *still* have a relatively high blood concentration on Wednesday. Although more research is needed in this area, the individual may not be impaired on Wednesday. Second, it is not easy to obtain blood tests in the field. Specialized personnel must be transported to the scene of accidents to draw blood in order to make the most accurate assessment of driving impairment.

The lack of good testing technology for law enforcement, combined with a lack of good data on what constitutes marijuana-impaired driving, should give everyone reason to think. As we move to decriminalize or legalize recreational marijuana use, what is a "safe" amount in the body while driving? The difficulty in determining this could mean we see an increase in impaired drivers. Public safety—as well as a concern for uniform and fair enforcement of the law—would suggest we proceed down this path with caution.

My Position on Decriminalization of Marijuana

My personal position is that it is reasonable to consider occasional, recreational use of marijuana by adults—especially those above the age of twenty-five whose brains are no longer developing—in a manner similar (though not the same) as we consider the occasional, recreational use of alcohol. This means that I agree with the idea of decriminalizing possession of small amounts of marijuana intended for the use of the person who obtained it. If people are able to use marijuana like this in a "responsible fashion"—without affecting their own immediate safety or the health and safety of anyone else— then such use should not be subject to a criminal penalty. In these instances, using law enforcement resources to prevent people from indulging in the recreational use of marijuana is not necessary. As noted previously, there's a lot of social and personal expense—in tax dollars, personal income, and degradation of "social capital"—when we devote our limited resources to criminalizing behavior that has low risk. So, for this reason, I support decriminalization—to a point. Unfortunately, marijuana decriminalization laws are an excellent example of how ideas can be conceptually sound, but their implementation can be problematic. The chief problem with marijuana decriminalization laws, however, is the way statutes define "small amounts" of marijuana. Most decriminalization laws define a small amount of marijuana as being less than one ounce. We would leave the table pretty hungry if someone served us a one-ounce steak, but in the case of marijuana, it's a huge helping—enough for five weeks of nearly daily use. Marijuana is a dried plant product, so an ounce is a significant amount (see figure 3). According to the World Health Organization, a typical marijuana joint contains a half gram of marijuana.[37] That means an ounce of marijuana can be used to roll up to fifty-six joints!

FIGURE 3. One ounce of marijuana

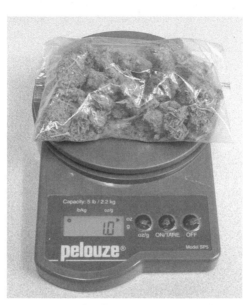

Photo courtesy of Norfolk, MA, District Attorney's Office

Most policymakers are shocked by this, because they think of an ounce as a small amount. In addition, most people don't buy marijuana by the ounce, either. An ounce of medium-grade marijuana typically costs about $300, with a high-grade ounce typically selling for $400. So most people will buy a much smaller amount—perhaps an eighth or a quarter of an ounce. (They will pay a little more for this—the price goes up as the amount gets smaller.) Generally, the lightest regular users—users who smoke about one joint a day—will use about one-eighth ounce of marijuana a week, making an "eighth" the amount most often purchased at one time. This further underscores the notion that people carrying around an ounce of marijuana probably have intentions for that marijuana beyond simply using it themselves.

I believe that the ounce limit associated with decriminalization of marijuana laws is the main problem with the laws. Again, there are many people who do not want to demonize adults who choose to possess and use a small amount of marijuana recreationally. But an ounce is not a small amount. If someone is caught carrying around three-fourths of an ounce of marijuana, enough to roll about forty joints, current decriminalization laws consider this as possession of "personal use" marijuana. This is flawed logic, because most people carrying enough marijuana to roll forty joints could easily be interested in selling it. If the possession limit for these laws was adjusted to one-fourth of an ounce, for example, the limit would be closer to what could reasonably be associated with personal use. Those carrying more would be treated criminally, assuming that marijuana remains illegal in that state. So the *idea* of decriminalization is a good one, but the implementation thus far has not been optimal. Sadly, this is a common theme in marijuana policy to date; the policies don't seem grounded in the logic of public health.

My Position on Legalization of the Recreational Use of Marijuana

If forced to vote right now, I would not support legalization of the recreational use of marijuana. One reason is that the issue of drugged driving has not been addressed sufficiently to this point—we do not have a practical method of testing for marijuana impairment that is on par with what is currently available for alcohol. In addition, I would like to evaluate data from the states that have already legalized recreational use with respect to addiction and other potential societal costs before making my decision. I do think the legalization of the recreational use of marijuana is feasible with an appropriate set of regulations. If the voting public is well educated on the issues related to marijuana and decides that they want to legalize it, this can be done in a way that largely limits the risk involved. I don't think, however, that we currently have the knowledge necessary to implement legalization as safely as we might be able to, and this is related to some of the potential negative consequences of marijuana that we have already discussed.

Some in favor of these laws may resign themselves to accepting the cost of increased use by young people if it comes with perceived benefits of the laws. I would like to believe, however, that if we are going to enact these laws, we as a society could do a better job of limiting young people's access to marijuana. To accomplish this, however, more stakeholders need to be at the table when regulations are written.

The implementation of legalization in Washington and Colorado provides a couple of case studies that we must pay extra attention to. Ideally, we would have several years to watch things play out in these states—both what went well and what did not—before we evaluate the evidence and decide whether to move forward and, if so, how to do so in a way that minimizes risk. Of course, we need to see how legalization affects the addiction rates in Washington and Colorado. We should also evaluate several other practical matters that these states are addressing right now, such as how the stores will operate, the packaging of marijuana-infused edible products, and advertising. While legalization is an idea worth considering, the implementation thus far in Washington and Colorado is worrisome—there are issues that should be sorted out before more states legalize recreational use.

As a researcher who conducts clinical trials that have the potential to be both beneficial and harmful to patients, I hold a belief in the scientific process that affects how I look at the issue of legalization. I am forced to balance a set of risks and benefits, and while they lean against legalization at the moment, they may shift in favor of legalization as we gather more data. While there are some people who seem to be either for or against legalization "no matter what," I am not one of those people. As much as is possible, this should be a decision based on evidence. Public policy changes are experiments in social behavior, and we are always collecting data. My hope is that this book will illustrate the importance of evaluating the data critically in as balanced a fashion as possible and making informed decisions based upon the evidence.

There is still time before legalization of recreational marijuana makes it onto the ballot in most states. The issues described above are not set in stone; there are many steps we can take to obtain a lucid picture of what legalization might mean. Massachusetts, for example, seems likely to contest the question of legalization in November 2016. That is more than a year and a half from when this book will be published, meaning there is still time to conduct important research and determine answers that will help people decide how they want to vote, while also evaluating data from states that have already decided to legalize the drug.

Summary

Decriminalization of marijuana and legalization of the recreational use of marijuana, along with medical marijuana, are the major legal issues related to marijuana in the United States. The question of legalization has jumped to the front of the line as the first four states—Washington, Colorado, Alaska, and Oregon—as well as the District of Columbia have now voted to legalize the recreational use of marijuana. And several more are debating whether or not they should follow. As of this writing, seventeen states (and DC) have decriminalized possession of small quantities of marijuana intended for one's personal use. While such possession is still illegal, those caught with less than a stipulated amount—usually one ounce—are subject only to a civil fine as opposed to a criminal charge.

Legalization of the recreational use of marijuana entails treating marijuana like alcohol. Only those age twenty-one and older are allowed to buy it, they may buy it from marijuana stores, and this marijuana is taxed at the state level. However, the issue of legalizing the recreational use of marijuana isn't black or white, and one can make a strong argument in either direction. If legalized, marijuana would be treated as a commodity, which means that there would be legal production, distribution, sale, and possession. The case studies of other legal substances, alcohol and tobacco, are important to consider: While they are heavily taxed, use of alcohol and nicotine results in tremendous health and societal costs.

Basic arguments for decriminalization and legalization include increased personal liberty, financial benefits, reduced black market, difficulty enforcing criminal penalties, and decreased incarceration, particularly of minorities, related to marijuana possession. The fundamental argument against decriminalization and, to a larger degree, legalization is that these laws will increase access to and use of marijuana, particularly among young people. In addition, there are concerns that decriminalization and legalization of marijuana will repeat the negative aspects of our history with nicotine and alcohol, result in increased driving under the influence of marijuana, and remove the deterrent effect that the illegal status of marijuana currently provides.

I agree with the concept underlying decriminalization of marijuana: that possession of small amounts of marijuana should not result in criminal charges that run the risk of bogging down our legal system. However, decriminalization laws would be improved with a lower limit for what constitutes "personal use" marijuana. Lowering the limit to one-fourth ounce would be an improvement over current laws, as someone carrying around one ounce in public is likely selling it to others.

My position on legalizing marijuana for recreational use is that it is feasible, provided there are appropriate regulations in place to limit the marijuana-related risks. I would like to see additional research done on marijuana-impaired driving, and we should also carefully study the effects that legalization is having in the states that have already implemented it before we legalize recreational use elsewhere in the United States.

7

Medical Marijuana

THE SCIENCE AND PRACTICAL IMPLICATIONS

Public opinion in the United States has shifted in the past twenty years in favor of the use of medical marijuana. California was the first state to enact medical marijuana laws in 1996, and as of this writing twenty-three states and the District of Columbia have passed laws to implement medical marijuana programs. Like seemingly all issues related to marijuana, medical marijuana—more specifically, the science supporting medical marijuana—has been hotly debated in recent years as the topic has made its way onto the ballot in state after state.

Thus, it is important to understand the pros and cons of medical marijuana from a theoretical standpoint. Researchers around the world recognize that marijuana and marijuana-like drugs in the cannabinoid family have tremendous medical potential. Cutting-edge cannabinoid research is taking place on a daily basis. As a result, new scientific data is published frequently, making the state of the scientific evidence for the medical uses of cannabinoids a moving target. In this chapter, you'll learn about the current state of the research on medical marijuana. This can help us see the potential benefits and harms that can come from legalizing marijuana's use as a medical product.

How Cannabinoids Work in the Body

The pharmacology of marijuana is responsible for its considerable therapeutic potential. Marijuana is made up of more than sixty different related chemicals called "cannabinoids," and those cannabinoids determine exactly what effects result from using the plant.[38] When a person uses marijuana and cannabinoids, the drug takes effect by plugging into cannabinoid receptors throughout the body. In a "lock and key" model, the cannabinoids are the keys, fitting into receptors located on nerve cells. These receptors are the locks, and this interaction results in the drug's effect, such as feeling "high" or experiencing reduced coordination. Figure 4 shows how these receptors work in the brain.

There are two main types of cannabinoid receptors: CB1 and CB2. CB1 receptors are located throughout the body, but they are concentrated heavily in the brain. CB2 receptors are mostly located throughout the arms and legs—what is referred to as the "periphery"—but there are some CB2 receptors in the brain as well.

The two main cannabinoids, or active ingredients, in marijuana are delta-9-tetrahydrocannabinol, also called THC, and cannabidiol, or CBD. THC and CBD are responsible for the effects that we typically associate with marijuana. There are many other cannabinoids, and some of them may prove to play important roles as medications or in marijuana's medicinal effects. But right now, the two key cannabinoids that we know the most about are THC and CBD. THC is the "psychoactive" ingredient, meaning it is what produces the euphoria or high that comes from using marijuana. And, it is THC that can produce psychosis in the small number of people who are vulnerable to this effect. Psychosis is defined as the feeling that a person is experiencing things that are not actually happening, such as hearing or seeing things that are not there.

FIGURE 4. Cannabinoids plug in to receptor sites in brain cells

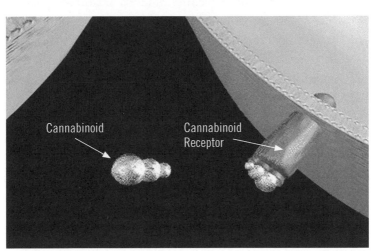

Cannabinoid

Cannabinoid
Receptor

Adapted from an image from the National Institute on Drug Abuse, National Institutes of Health

CBD is not psychoactive, but it does have a calming, or anti-anxiety effect, and increasing amounts of research point to CBD having antipsychotic effects as well in reducing the frequency and severity of psychotic symptoms.[39]

CBD may also have properties that help to reduce seizures. Many people have been talking about CBD recently as a potential treatment for patients with seizure disorders or epilepsy, who have not responded to traditional antiseizure medications. In 2013, Dr. Sanjay Gupta, a brain surgeon and medical correspondent for CNN, chronicled the heartbreaking story of a young child with Dravet syndrome, a seizure disorder typically found in infants and children that can result in hundreds of seizures per day. As the child grows, the seizures disrupt his or her quality of life, causing developmental delays, movement issues, sleep disruption, and many other problems. Dravet syndrome has proved difficult to treat thus far, and Dr. Gupta's television show stirred up a great deal of support for medical marijuana as the child's family shared their story of successfully using marijuana strains with high concentrations of CBD to fight their daughter's seizures. Clinical trials of CBD as a treatment for seizure disorders are ongoing in the United States today.

The concentration of THC or CBD—that is, amount of THC in comparison to CBD—determines the effects of a particular strain of marijuana. Therefore, it is important to know the concentrations of THC and CBD in any marijuana that is used. The technology of growing marijuana—using powerful lights and the best soil, for example—has improved by leaps and bounds in recent years. Before growing technology improved to its current level, marijuana usually contained roughly equal concentrations of THC and CBD. Today, technology allows growers to adjust the concentrations of THC and CBD in their marijuana to produce a desired effect, and this is a way to distinguish types of marijuana from each other in a crowded, competitive marketplace. THC concentrations are directly related to CBD concentrations; increasing THC typically results in *lower* CBD concentrations, while decreasing THC results in *higher* CBD concentrations. Strains of marijuana with high THC concentrations can produce more powerful highs, while strains of marijuana with high concentrations of CBD may be better in treating seizure and other disorders.

Once again, it is important to point out that today's marijuana is very different from the marijuana that many of us grew up with in the 1960s, 1970s, and 1980s. In those decades, the average THC content was about 1–2 percent. The latest average THC content established in the United States is 13 percent, meaning that marijuana bought today is usually at least six times stronger (more potent) than in previous decades.[40] Also, keep in mind that marijuana with a THC content in the range of 27 percent can be purchased—that's fourteen times more potent than marijuana of decades past.

Proven and Potential Medicinal Uses

Marijuana has a fascinating history as a medication, having been used over the past 5,000 years for a host of medical purposes, as noted in chapter 1. It has played a role as an important medicine in societies all over the world, and it has had a prominent medical role in the United States since colonial times. By the 1850s, marijuana was used as an appetite stimulant as well as an agent that suppressed nausea and vomiting. Marijuana was a part of several medications until it was made illegal by the federal government in 1937. Marijuana, the plant, has remained illegal since that time, but studies of the medicinal properties of both marijuana and cannabinoids have continued.

FDA-approved cannabinoid drugs

As of August 2014, there are two FDA-approved cannabinoid drugs: dronabinol, which is sold under the trade name Marinol, and nabilone, which is sold under the trade name Cesamet. Because they are members of the cannabinoid family, they are similar to marijuana in many ways and produce many similar effects. Between research supported by government agencies like the National Institutes of Health and the pharmaceutical companies interested in establishing proven uses for these medications, dronabinol and nabilone have been studied extensively. After a lengthy, rigorous process, dronabinol and nabilone each earned two indications, or FDA endorsements: the first for nausea and vomiting typically associated with cancer chemotherapy, and the second for appetite stimulation in wasting illnesses where patients have difficulty eating, such as human immunodeficiency virus (HIV).

These indications are relevant to the medical marijuana discussion because they eliminate some patients' need for medical marijuana. The patient may benefit from one of the cannabinoid drugs rather than marijuana. If patients, for example, become

interested in getting a medical marijuana certification in order
to treat nausea or vomiting, their doctor will likely provide a
prescription for one of these two FDA-approved medications
instead.

Why do we need cannabinoid drugs when we can use marijuana?

An important question is why would we spend time developing cannabinoid drugs like dronabinol and nabilone when we
already have marijuana? There are several important medical
reasons that are separate from any reasons involving policy,
personal choice, profit, or other divisive issues. First, remember
that marijuana contains many types of cannabinoids as well
as other compounds. So the person who ingests the marijuana
plant, whether by smoking, eating, or other methods, is taking
in many other compounds, some of which may not be beneficial, may be harmful, or may cause undesired side effects. We
have used this same model with many other medicines that first
were derived from plants: we identify the useful compounds,
isolate them, and learn to manufacture and improve upon them.
Second, when we manufacture a compound, we can carefully
control its dose. This means that if we don't get the dose right
at first, we can adjust it readily. In a natural product—even one
where growers carefully breed different strains—it is difficult
to measure and control the dosage. It is hard to know just how
much of the desired chemical you're getting. So if the medicine
doesn't work right, it's hard to tell if the dosage was wrong or
if something else was at fault. Third, when we gain control over
the compound, we can create it in other forms that may be more
beneficial and safer or may enable us to lead more productive
lives. Time release, a medication capsule designed to slowly
degrade over time, thereby exposing the body to medicine in a
steady, gradual fashion as opposed to an entire dose of medi-

cation at once, is a good example of this. Fourth, in the case of smoking medical marijuana, inhaling any kind of smoke into the lungs can cause cancer, emphysema, and other respiratory problems as well as heart disease, depending on the toxins in the smoke, making doctors reluctant to advise a patient to use the drug in this way.

The potential for cannabinoids in treating pain and MS

Many medications in the cannabinoid family, including dronabinol, nabilone, and marijuana—both smoked marijuana and in oral form—have been tested as treatments for a variety of illnesses in approximately fifty clinical trials. The results from these trials vary widely, as does the evidence for cannabinoids' effectiveness in the treatment of these illnesses.

Beyond nausea and appetite stimulation, the strongest evidence supporting the use of cannabinoids as a medication is for treating two other types of medical conditions. First is for use in treating pain: *chronic pain,* long-lasting pain that does not respond well to treatment, and *neuropathic pain,* pain from specific nerves that often leads to coldness or burning. Second, cannabinoids may be useful in treating the muscle spasticity, or tightness, associated with multiple sclerosis.

There have been ten studies looking at cannabinoids as treatments for chronic pain, and five of these studies have produced positive results. There have been six studies for cannabinoids as treatments for neuropathic pain, and three of these studies had positive results. There have been more than thirty trials examining cannabinoids as treatments for problems associated with multiple sclerosis; seventeen of these studies looked at spasticity associated with multiple sclerosis. These studies have shown that cannabinoids reduced spasticity, especially in the cases where the patients were asked to monitor and report changes in their spasticity themselves.[41]

Although several of these studies were positive, the FDA has not approved the use of any cannabinoids for pain or spasticity—yet. Pharmaceutical companies are working to gain FDA approvals for cannabinoids they are marketing for additional medical problems, including pain and spasticity. It seems likely that there will be new cannabinoids available in the next few years that have been FDA approved for treating medical problems beyond nausea, vomiting, and poor appetite.

So although there is evidence to use cannabinoids for these reasons, it is not overwhelmingly strong. In cases where patients and their doctors have exhausted all other available options, however, it would be reasonable to have a discussion about the risks and benefits of using a cannabinoid as a medication, despite the lack of FDA approval. It is worth noting that doctors routinely prescribe medications that do not have FDA approval for a particular purpose—we call it "off-label" prescribing. While I try to avoid doing this, I prescribe medications off-label if an FDA-approved medication (1) has already been tried without success or (2) has a bad side-effect profile that makes the off-label medication more appealing.

The Downsides of Medical Marijuana

The FDA-approved medications have several advantages over medical marijuana, mostly related to both quality control—meaning you are certain what is contained in a pill manufactured under FDA standards—and route of administration—most doctors would not recommend that a patient smoke a medication. But people are using medical marijuana to treat many more problems besides nausea and poor appetite. Medical marijuana laws in the United States specifically mention a host of medical illnesses, including cancer, glaucoma, HIV, hepatitis C, ALS (also known as Lou Gehrig's disease), Crohn's disease, Parkinson's disease, and multiple sclerosis. The crucial question here is, "Is there strong science to support the use of medical marijuana for these illnesses?"

For the many illnesses mentioned in medical marijuana laws around the country, the data from scientific studies is weak or even nonexistent. There have been two clinical trials testing cannabinoids for glaucoma, and while these medications have properties that would be useful for treating glaucoma, the positive aspects of these studies are not strong enough to outweigh the side effects of marijuana. As a result, most eye doctors, as well as the Glaucoma Research Foundation, do not recommend the use of cannabinoids, including marijuana, as medications for glaucoma.[42] A handful of clinical trials looked at the use of cannabinoids as treatment for Parkinson's disease and hepatitis C, and these trials did not produce positive results. There have also been a small number of studies for using cannabinoids to treat cancer pain and HIV-related problems such as depression and insomnia. While these studies were negative, many cancer and HIV patients have nausea or poor appetite, and it's clear that cannabinoids can be helpful for treating those issues—but not for HIV itself.

As mentioned earlier, ALS is listed in the medical marijuana laws in many states, and yet there has been only one clinical trial examining cannabinoids as medications for ALS and it didn't have positive results.[43] The limited amount of research looking at cannabinoids as treatments for ALS compared to its widespread application illustrates the dangerous position we are in regarding medical marijuana laws in the United States. The policy is ahead of the science. Medicine does not work this way—in medicine, we aim to establish the safety and effectiveness of treatments *before* we recommend them to large numbers of people. The studies show a shockingly wide range of results when testing cannabinoids like marijuana as medications for these serious medical conditions. Therefore, while it may be reasonable to consider cannabinoids for some of these illnesses when other treatment options have been exhausted, it is disturbing to think that some patients may be relying on medical marijuana when better, potentially life-saving alternatives exist.

Due to the lack of clinical trials or the inconclusive or negative results of the studies that have been completed, few major medical organizations endorse the use of medical marijuana. The American Medical Association, the American Psychiatric Association, the American Academy of Addiction Psychiatry, the American Society of Addiction Medicine, and the American Academy of Child and Adolescent Psychiatry all have released position papers outlining why they do not support medical marijuana. Psychiatrists Dr. Herbert Kleber and Dr. Robert DuPont summarized the concerns of many doctors in their 2012 commentary, which appeared in the *American Journal of Psychiatry*, one of the top medical journals in the country: "Medical marijuana laws challenge physicians to recommend use of a Schedule I illegal drug of abuse with no scientific approval, dosage control, or quality control."[44]

These concerns are among those leading to the current situation, where most doctors are not eager to recommend medical marijuana for their patients. Imagine the difficulties doctors might face if something went wrong with a patient to whom they had recommended the use of an illegal, non-FDA-approved drug as medication.

There are two small "windows" in which it makes sense to consider medical marijuana. In both instances, every effort should be made to use traditional medical methods—some involving medications and some not—before considering medical marijuana. The first window is for medical problems such as chronic pain, neuropathic pain, and spasticity associated with multiple sclerosis. As we have shown, the data supporting the use of medical marijuana for these illnesses is positive enough to *consider* marijuana as a possible treatment—but it is not overwhelmingly positive. The second window is for medical illnesses where cannabidiol (CBD) or other cannabinoids may be helpful in treating a disease entity. For example, animal studies have suggested that CBD may be effective in reducing seizures in patients where conventional medications have not done so.[45] This has led some patients and parents of children with seizure disorders—like the child with Dravet syndrome discussed earlier—to seek marijuana containing high concentrations of CBD and, subsequently, has resulted in clinical trials of CBD as a treatment for seizure disorders.

In instances where it may make sense to consider medical marijuana as a treatment, no doctor is likely to recommend that patients smoke it. The standard policy is, since no FDA-approved medication is smoked, medical marijuana should not be smoked. The main reason for this is that smoking harms our lungs and is not a safe way to take a medicine. Drugs are smoked as a way for people to feel their effects more quickly, just as some choose to inject drugs for a nearly instantaneous effect. Injecting any kind of medication has at least some risk, which is why intravenous medications and fluids are administered at hospitals under the supervision of highly trained medical professionals. If patients are relying on medical marijuana for legitimate medical purposes—and a number of health care professionals maintain that many patients are not—then patients should be able to ingest marijuana and wait to feel the effects in the same way we wait minutes to feel the effect of aspirin or ibuprofen.

Research examining the effects of newer cannabinoids may eventually make medical marijuana (the plant) obsolete. CBD, for example, is already approved for use in other countries, and pharmaceutical companies are working hard right now to get it approved by the FDA. If CBD is approved by the FDA, then it would be safer for patients and doctors who feel CBD might be helpful for a specific medical problem to use the FDA-approved medication, which, unlike medical marijuana, offers a medicine of a known composition and purity. As more and more research is done showing that cannabinoids are effective treatments for medical problems, there should be less of a need to rely upon medical marijuana.

The Pros and Cons of Medical Marijuana

There are strong arguments both for and against medical marijuana, some of which we discussed in the previous chapter. The main argument for medical marijuana is that it provides access to a medication that may treat medical problems effectively. Often, those who become interested in exploring the merits of medical marijuana have had unsuccessful experiences treating diseases using multiple methods, including medications and other treatments that don't involve medications. They want to have the option to try medical marijuana as a possible treatment for an illness that has resisted other treatments without having to worry about potential legal consequences. Enacting medical marijuana laws also legitimizes the process of using marijuana medicinally, and having medical marijuana dispensaries regulated by state governments should make the process safer for patients—and profitable for the state from a tax perspective. Another argument for medical marijuana is that the use of medical marijuana may lead to less use of powerful opioid medications in patients who suffer from chronic pain, should research confirm its effectiveness.

The main argument against medical marijuana is concern about increased access to marijuana, especially for young people. As we discussed in the previous chapter, more people using marijuana, even for medicinal purposes, will likely mean that more people will become addicted to marijuana. Addiction and other adverse health effects come at a cost to both the individual and society. The morality of using marijuana is another argument—many Americans simply think that marijuana is bad and that no one should ever use it. These folks do not care if the purpose of marijuana is medicinal or recreational; they oppose it no matter what. Others who are against medical marijuana say that physicians should stick to the FDA-approved cannabinoids and that the data does not support the use of medical marijuana for most of the disease entities for which people intend to use it as a treatment.

Troubling Consequences of Medical Marijuana Laws

While there has been intense debate about the scientific rationale for medical marijuana, most involved would agree that the implementation of medical marijuana laws has been challenging. This drives home the point that while an idea may be a good one, the way in which that idea is executed may not be. Those who are in favor of medical marijuana often feel that the regulations are too restrictive, keeping medical marijuana out of the hands of those who need it to treat serious medical illnesses. On the other hand, those who are against medical marijuana often feel that the laws are not restrictive enough, resulting in medical marijuana ending up in the hands of people without significant medical illnesses. Both arguments have some truth.

The implementation of medical marijuana laws in Massachusetts, where I treat patients, is a good example of the frustration felt by those on both sides of this legal debate. In November 2012, 63 percent of Massachusetts residents voted in favor of medical marijuana. Leading up to the vote, advertisements in support of medical marijuana told of the importance of making medical marijuana accessible to those with "debilitating" medical illnesses that significantly affected quality of life. Organizations and coalitions opposed to medical marijuana attempted to spread the word about the potential harms of marijuana, especially to young people who begin using marijuana regularly while their brain is still developing.

Medical marijuana laws were voted in overwhelmingly; some were elated and others were disappointed. The sentiment of the Massachusetts voters, however, seemed to echo the sentiments of a growing number of Americans, so it is important to try to understand why public opinion is shifting in favor of medical marijuana. When we consider the overwhelming support for medical marijuana, and the question of legalizing the drug, for that matter, it may be helpful to keep these three other words in mind: *easier, stronger, cheaper.* These are the reasons that people who use marijuana occasionally for recreational purposes would support medical marijuana or legalization of marijuana. Marijuana is everywhere. And while it is very easy to find and to buy, it stands to reason that recreational users would be in favor of laws that make it easier to get. The quality and strength of marijuana has increased along with improving technology and interest in growing it, which has accompanied medical marijuana efforts. Recreational users prefer stronger, higher-grade marijuana, so they will likely vote for laws that would encourage further improvement of marijuana's quality and potency. Finally, an ounce of high-grade marijuana costs $400 right now in Massachusetts—an ounce of similar high-grade marijuana in Colorado, where both medical marijuana and recreational marijuana is legal, is $150. Nobody wants to pay more money than they have to, so recreational users are going to support laws that result in price reduction.

For those opposed to medical marijuana, the laws are not restrictive enough. In Massachusetts, for example, the Department of Public Health regulations state that medical marijuana is intended for people with one of eight debilitating conditions— cancer, glaucoma, HIV, hepatitis C, ALS, Crohn's disease, Parkinson's disease, or multiple sclerosis.[46] However, physicians' recommendations are not limited to these eight conditions—they can recommend medical marijuana for whatever medical problem they choose. The result is that many people receive medical marijuana recommendations who do not have one of the debilitating conditions. A simple way to rectify this would be to use a system similar to a medical prior authorization system. Your doctor sometimes must file paperwork with your insurance company in order to prescribe newer, more expensive medications when cheaper alternatives are available. Prior authorization systems have been shown to reduce unnecessary prescribing of expensive medications—doctors change their prescribing behaviors when they know they have to jump through hoops.[47] A similar system for medical marijuana would decrease the likelihood that medical marijuana ends up in the hands of patients who may not need it.

Another problem with medical marijuana laws is the amount of marijuana allowed. In Massachusetts, for example, a doctor is permitted to recommend ten ounces or even more per sixty days. This is an enormous amount of marijuana. The *heavy* marijuana users in my clinical trials smoke an average of a half ounce per week, which translates into four ounces in a sixty-day period. It is hard to imagine, therefore, a patient needing ten ounces every sixty days. In Massachusetts, individuals whose income levels qualify them for welfare are granted a hardship exception that allows them to grow their own marijuana. With such high sixty-day limits in place, it's feasible that patients who live in poverty will sell excess marijuana for profit. And when marijuana sells on the street for $300–$400 an ounce, it is hard to turn down such an opportunity. This is one likely contributor in a recent study that found Colorado medical marijuana ending up in the hands of adolescents who are in treatment for substance abuse.[48]

Despite problematic medical marijuana regulations in some states, medical marijuana is here to stay and clinicians need to be comfortable evaluating whether medical marijuana is appropriate for specific patients and discussing these options with patients and colleagues.[49] Some of my colleagues have dismissed medical marijuana as a sham—just a step on the pathway to legalization—and don't want anything to do with it. I have urged them to look at this as an opportunity to educate people about medical marijuana and, perhaps, even get some people treatment for addiction where they otherwise would not have received it.

Determining a patient's appropriateness for medical marijuana involves a careful, thoughtful evaluation. Lengthy evaluations are hard to come by in today's health care environment, so a thorough evaluation can uncover many issues overlooked during short visits. In such an evaluation, I want to know about patients' previous experiences with marijuana and what medical problem they hope it will treat. Due to marijuana's addictive potential and its negative effects on other psychiatric problems patients may have, their history of psychiatric problems and substance use must be addressed thoughtfully. Because of marijuana's unpredictable psychoactive effects on patients with psychiatric problems, these patients are *not* good candidates for medical marijuana.

In the course of learning about patients' medical history, current medications, allergies, family history, and social history, I also ask patients if there are recent psychosocial stressors that may complicate medical marijuana therapy. This is the same process a physician should use when prescribing other mood-altering drugs. For example, when I prescribe other medications, like benzodiazepines, with abuse potential and the potential for significant side effects, I have the patient stay in closer contact with me by phone and follow-up appointments than I would otherwise.

Because pain and multiple sclerosis spasticity are the areas where the best case for medical marijuana can typically be made, I recommend that the doctor treating these problems—or any of the other debilitating conditions marijuana is intended to treat—write the certification. This is preferred over having a doctor in a medical marijuana clinic write the certification, because patients are more likely to follow up with their own oncologist or neurologist.

While the science does not provide strong support for the use of medical marijuana at present, medical marijuana programs are still feasible. If voted in, reasonable plans that lessen the risk will need to be implemented. Rather than having the distribution of medical marijuana blossom into a billion-dollar industry, a much smaller program aimed at distributing medical marijuana only to patients with debilitating conditions should be the goal. As an example of what can go wrong, Colorado passed an amendment allowing medical marijuana in 2000. According to a 2011 story in the *Huffington Post,* by 2011 Denver had more medical marijuana dispensaries than it had Starbucks coffee shops.[50] It seems very unlikely that there is a greater medical need for marijuana in Denver than the recreational consumption of coffee products. This is evidence that medical marijuana is probably being redirected for recreational use. While medical marijuana should be feasible, the implementation thus far in the United States does not inspire confidence.

Summary

Marijuana has had a long and fascinating history as a medicine in societies around the globe. In the United States, marijuana had an important role as a medication until it was made illegal in 1937. There are two cannabinoids available in the United States now that are FDA approved for nausea and vomiting associated with cancer chemotherapy as well as appetite stimulation in wasting illnesses. However, there is a strong desire in the United States to use medical marijuana as a treatment for a host of other diseases. For some of these disease entities—chronic pain, neuropathic pain, and spasticity associated with multiple sclerosis—there is fairly strong evidence supporting the use of medical marijuana as an effective treatment, albeit not a first- or second-line treatment. For many other diseases, the evidence supporting the use of medical marijuana as a treatment is weak. It is important to note that the results of current research and the availability of medications that may obtain FDA approval in the next few years may change the need for medical marijuana as a treatment in the United States. Right now, though, access to medical marijuana is necessary, as there is reasonable scientific evidence that suggests the marijuana plant may provide medicinal benefits that are not attainable with the current array of FDA-approved medications.

Difficulties in implementation of medical marijuana laws, though, coupled with concerning national trends toward increased marijuana misuse, make it hard to imagine that the rates of marijuana misuse and addiction won't get worse before they improve. It is my hope that a thoughtful discussion will enable us to learn from early implementation problems as we move forward together.

SECTION IV

TREATMENT

8

Never Worry Alone

FINDING HELP FOR SOMEONE
WHO MAY HAVE A PROBLEM

Addiction is everywhere. Almost 15 percent of Americans—about one of every seven of us—will struggle with an addiction during their lifetime.[51] It is hard to watch the news on television or read the newspaper without seeing a story about addiction and its consequences. It may not be the feature story because at times we still are hesitant to talk about addiction, but the story is there if you look for it. Similarly, the statistics of addiction and its staggering prevalence—how many people are struggling with addiction at any one time—suggests that we all know family or friends who have such problems. If you cannot think of someone you know with an addiction, you may not be thinking hard enough.

Knowing someone who has battled addiction and knowing how to help someone with addiction are entirely different things. Addiction can manifest itself in a number of ways that cover a wide spectrum. Unless you have experienced the terrible toll that addiction can take on people and their families, it is hard to appreciate the extent of the wreckage addiction can cause. For example, opioid addiction generally presents itself in spectacular, dramatic fashion. People addicted to opioids might overdose on heroin and nearly die, or they might attempt to rob a pharmacy for prescription opioid painkillers like oxycodone. Marijuana addiction is often much more difficult to detect due to the tendency for the person to show more subtle signs of addiction.

Chris

Chris, a sixteen-year-old high school sophomore, just hadn't been acting like "his normal self" over the past few months. He decided not to play soccer this fall, despite having played the sport since he was seven, and his grades continued to drift downward. At home, he was much more isolated than usual, spending most of his time locked in his room playing video games and listening to music. Chris seemed to spend less time with his childhood friends, including those who still went to the same school he did, and, when he did spend time with others, it was with a new group of friends. His parents and younger sister noticed this change and were worried about it. Attempts to talk to Chris about his change in behavior, however, were met with a stance that was at times defensive or, at other times, evasive. This troubling pattern continued for months until his mother, while trying to address the growing piles of clothes in Chris's room—one thing that hadn't changed—found a small bag of marijuana in a pair of pants. With a sense of dread and panic, Chris's mother called her husband and they frantically tried to decide what to do next.

Chris's marijuana use contributed to a slow and steady decline that would have been challenging for even a skilled counselor or doctor to notice. His changes in behavior (and the resulting decline in wellness) would have continued to be a mystery had his mother not uncovered the marijuana.

Signs and Symptoms of Marijuana Addiction

In chapter 4, we reviewed the ways in which marijuana addiction is very similar to addiction to other drugs, like alcohol and opioids. Marijuana use typically crosses over into addiction when a person is using daily or nearly every day. By that time, marijuana use will likely have produced a negative effect on at least one major area of that person's life, such as relationships, work, or school. Marijuana addiction also frequently results in changes in behavior and personality—a social, outgoing person becoming withdrawn, for example. Worsening grades or increased isolation may be a result of marijuana addiction, but it would take an astute observer to see one of these problems alone as grounds for asking about addiction issues. In my clinical experience, in part due to parents', teachers', family members', or spouses' unfamiliarity with signs and symptoms of marijuana addiction, it takes more than one of these problems to trigger someone to ask more questions about addiction. The case of Chris illustrates this nicely: his parents noted both a decline in grades and changing behaviors around the house. My hope is that this book will make it more likely for parents, school staff, spouses, friends, and even clinicians to detect marijuana addiction sooner, so that those addicted to marijuana will get the help they need sooner than they otherwise would.

Other common signs and symptoms of marijuana addiction are described in the *Diagnostic and Statistical Manual of Mental Disorders, 5th edition (DSM-5).*[52] These may also provide a tip-off to a marijuana problem. More important, these signs and symptoms may provide clues to a marijuana addiction problem in cases where there is no "smoking gun." Loved ones do not always observe someone using marijuana or find marijuana or marijuana-related items, so it is critical to at least be aware of how things might look if someone developed a problem with addiction. Some of the most common areas of concern where marijuana use might be a factor are social problems, reducing or giving up important activities, using in dangerous situations, and using despite psychological or physical problems. (Parents can turn to appendix B for a list of signs their child may be using.)

Social problems

People with marijuana addiction may fail to fulfill major obligations due to use, such as not showing up for work, or an appointment, or for a social event that they were supposed to attend. A usually responsible young adult, for example, may start missing all family activities without being able to provide a good reason.

Samantha

Samantha is a twenty-five-year-old woman with no previous psychiatric history who was referred to me by her boyfriend. Samantha graduated from college almost three years ago and dreamed of going to graduate school to become a clinical psychologist. When she was referred to me, though, she had yet to take the GREs and had been working at a seasonal novelty retail store for the past two years. Her boyfriend was worried about her marijuana use; they smoked together a couple of times per week in college, but he had since given up smoking while she had increased her use to smoking almost daily by herself. Recently, her boyfriend had noticed that Samantha was not interested in doing things that she usually enjoyed, namely volunteering at a local women's shelter and staying in touch with her family, who lived in a neighboring town.

Samantha stopped volunteering and communicating with her family in the way that she had previously. Family and friends usually are initially surprised by such behavior change, but if an addiction problem is not uncovered, missing family activities becomes the norm. A rift between the young adult and family often follows.

Important activities given up or reduced

Chris, in our example, stopped playing organized soccer after years of involvement in the sport. Another patient of mine played golf his entire life and continued to play several times a week into his mid-twenties while holding down a full-time job. At a point when his marijuana use escalated for a variety of reasons, he reduced his golf to a couple times per month. In hindsight, his family said that they wished they had noticed this shift in his behavior.

Use in dangerous situations

Marijuana use can be especially risky when it occurs in hazardous situations. Due in part to the difficulty in detecting marijuana addiction in some instances, the addiction may sometimes come to the surface only with risky use. For example, I have worked with patients whose parents realized that their child may have an addiction to marijuana after a second driving infraction involving the drug. Another patient was referred to me after she was observed smoking marijuana in a restroom at work. To put important parts of your life such as work and school in peril in order to use marijuana is a red flag that you might be addicted.

Use despite obvious physical or psychological problems

Marijuana use tends to be an issue when people fail to make the connection between their regular marijuana use and other significant problems they are experiencing. I have had many patients come to me wondering why their depression or anxiety was not responding to medications, only to discover that they were smoking marijuana daily. It is very difficult for an antidepressant to work as well as it can when someone is using marijuana regularly. As we reviewed in chapter 3, marijuana use has been linked to instances of increased anxiety and depression.

Is Marijuana the Problem?

Chris's and Samantha's cases illustrate that there are times when other problems surface before marijuana use has been identified as an issue. This can happen in a variety of scenarios. The decline in Chris's grades and his decision not to play soccer alone may have triggered concern on the part of his parents, perhaps resulting in an evaluation. It is challenging to detect addiction problems without a "smoking gun" or a catastrophic event like a car accident. Such spectacular events are less likely to occur with people using marijuana as opposed to those who are using opioids like heroin or oxycodone, for example. This is one reason that many people who have problems with marijuana never end up getting formal treatment.

These are some of the special challenges that teachers or employers face. They are less likely than loved ones to learn directly about someone's marijuana use by observing use or finding marijuana paraphernalia. As a result, teachers and employers are usually not the ones making referrals to clinicians like me. However, it is still important for teachers and employers to know what to look for in terms of signs and symptoms of marijuana addiction, so that they can act in cases where it appears as if someone is not doing well. Teachers and employers are well within their boundaries to ask the student or employee if there is a problem they can help the student or employee resolve. If the answer is affirmative, teachers can refer students to the school nurse or substance abuse coalition clinician, if available; employers can refer employees to employee assistance program officials.

How to Have "the Conversation"

There are four key steps to helping someone you care about find help for marijuana addiction. Preparation, conversation, evaluation, and referral all play a critical role in determining if structured treatment is necessary and placing someone into that treatment. Many people either avoid having the conversation with their loved one about their marijuana use or they jump into that conversation without a firm grasp on what they should say or what the possible outcomes may be.

Preparation

Identifying marijuana addiction and making an appropriate referral requires some preparation and knowledge of these steps ahead of time. It is important to have a sense for what the conversation, evaluation, and referral will look like before you begin those parts of the process. For a family member, teacher, or employer, the question of how to approach someone who you suspect has a marijuana problem is critical. Teachers, for example, risk losing credibility or losing the trust of their classroom overall if they don't handle these situations skillfully. Young teachers are often thrust into challenging situations very quickly, putting them in a difficult position because they often have had little or no training in how to handle such a predicament. These situations, however, can be pivotal, as they can shape how a given school year goes for both teachers and their students. Therefore, it is important to have an idea of how to handle such a situation before encountering it.

Before beginning the conversation about marijuana use, the following pieces should be in place. First, whoever initiates the conversation should have a previous relationship with the person, demonstrating an interest in his or her well-being. Second, have an idea of what you will say beforehand. Third, figure out how you will respond if the loved one wants help (if yes, you should have a professional in mind for the evaluation) and also what you will do if he or she does not.

Young people and adults who may have marijuana addiction will respond in many different ways when being approached about their marijuana use. Young people have fewer rights and there is a clear dynamic in which they are subordinates to parents, teachers, or other authority figures. Adults are less likely to be in subordinate positions where they feel they have to comply with the wishes of someone who is concerned about their use. Of course, there are some cases when employees are in subordinate positions and positive urine drug screens result in their employer recommending that they get an evaluation. In those cases, adults have little choice about what to do if they hope to keep their job. It is worth noting the differences between young people and adults in these situations, however, because the particular dynamic may change the amount of leverage the person approaching the marijuana user has.

People with a marijuana problem are more likely to be receptive to questions about their use if the concerned party has established an interest in their personal lives previously. This is a form of preparation—one must be in a position close enough to a person to allow for a sincere discussion about the person's marijuana use. Engaged parents, for example, who always ask about their child's day, despite at least superficial grumbling from the child, are in a better position to ask about important issues like drug use than parents who wait until major, often negative events, occur to show interest and concern. Kids are savvy about being able to tell who is truly interested in them and their daily activities, although they still may push back at times when parents ask. These interactions lay the groundwork, however, for the child feeling comfortable enough to approach or share when needed.

Conversation

Initial conversations work well when the parent, family member, or employer relays an important message. People who lead the initial conversation should send the message that *they want to preserve tangible things that a person has placed at risk with his or her marijuana use.* Kids are generally interested in what they can do to make sure that they will be able to do things like score well on standardized tests, avoid getting kicked out of school, or play in the sectional basketball game in two weeks.

Similarly, adults often want to save relationships or jobs that they have put in jeopardy with their marijuana use. It is worth noting, though, that while adults consciously believe they want to save relationships or jobs, these issues are usually more involved. They may be ambivalent about their job or relationship, meaning that part of them wants to stay in the relationship or job that is at risk, and part of them may not. That a part of them may not want to continue in the job or the relationship, often for long-simmering reasons, may explain why they have engaged in a behavior that has contributed to the precarious position they are in.

The second key message is to tell them (1) that you are concerned about them based on how you perceive things to be going for them lately and (2) that you think a professional evaluation is necessary. Establishing that you are interested in helping them preserve key aspects of their lives—school, work, or relationships—shows that you are on the same page with them and recognize the importance of what needs to be saved. The second message leads the way to help. The message should be clear: the person's current level of marijuana use is concerning to you. This clarity is especially important with young people, since research shows that regular marijuana use may affect their developing brain. Young people who frequently use marijuana may find it hard to understand any indirect, subtle, or abstract messages. By stating that you are concerned but not absolutely certain that the person's use has reached the level of addiction and that it is best for a qualified professional to make the determination of whether marijuana addiction is present, you can remain allied with the person because you will not be the one making a diagnosis. As mentioned above, there are different dynamics depending on who may have a problem (young person or adult) and whether the concerned party is a parent, teacher, or employer. The conversation should be framed so the person has a choice about what to do, although sometimes, such as when an employee must get an evaluation after a positive urine drug screen, this is clearly not possible.

A question sometimes arises about whether an authority, such as the school or employer, should be notified about a person's marijuana use. The parent, friend, teacher, or co-worker approaching the person who may have a problem wants the person to do well and is not trying to get that person punished in an official capacity. For that reason, the concerned party is often worried that his or her actions may bring a suspension or even job loss. In most cases, schools and employers genuinely want people to get help for their problem so that they can function well as students and employees. There usually are personal connections present that make this more likely. For these reasons, I recommend that schools and employers be informed, especially if school or work will be missed or if the school's or employer's involvement may bring additional treatment resources. If marijuana users have a legitimate issue related to their use, the school or employer will likely find out eventually, and it is better to be told about a problem rather than discover it on their own.

After a person recognizes that help is necessary, figuring out the next step can be overwhelming. Unless someone has had the unfortunate experience of having a loved one struggle with addiction, it is nearly impossible to know the practical steps necessary to help someone who needs help for an addiction. Therefore, I suggest keeping this next critical step as simple as possible.

Never worry alone

Have your help lined up *before* you begin the conversation. While it is not realistic to expect someone to know the steps necessary to access help or what different levels of treatment may be available before reading a book like this, knowing whom to call is an easier question to address. Have an idea about whom to call before approaching the person who may have a problem, for when it comes to addiction, windows of opportunity open and close quickly and you must be ready to take advantage of an opportunity. Call your doctor, the school nurse, or a treatment center that specializes in addiction. There are many people who want the best for you and your family, and these people have the knowledge needed to direct you to the necessary services.

While there are myriad types of treatment, the crucial first step is to get the person with a problem to talk to someone knowledgeable about addiction. This should take the form of a thorough initial evaluation by a therapist—typically a substance abuse counselor, social worker, psychologist, primary care doctor, or psychiatrist. A primary care doctor will likely refer you to one of the other four other types of clinicians mentioned above, but some doctors will do the evaluation themselves. Most people with addiction problems do not seek treatment, and those with marijuana addiction are no different. Remember, for the reasons discussed in earlier chapters, many Americans do not think of marijuana addiction as something that would require treatment. As a result, those with marijuana problems often need strong encouragement just to get an initial evaluation, but this is a vital step.

What Happens at an Evaluation

When clients come into my office for an initial evaluation of their marijuana use, I know that at least a small part of them acknowledges that there is a problem. People who seek help from health care professionals on their own are more motivated and usually fare better than those who are pressured into getting help, but it doesn't have to be this way. Someone guided into treatment by family, friends, school, or employers can also do well.

In my office, an initial evaluation of marijuana use takes about seventy-five minutes and, if a loved one brought the person in, I spend the final twenty to thirty minutes with both the client and his or her loved one so that my recommendations are clear and we are all on the same page moving forward. In my private practice, marijuana is identified as a likely problem, often the main problem, in most of the evaluations I do. Marijuana addiction can be uncovered during evaluations of other psychiatric problems like anxiety or depression, but since I specialize in treating people with marijuana addiction, marijuana use is often not a secret by the time patients see me.

During the evaluation, I have four goals. The first goal is to have patients tell me one reason why they want to change their marijuana use. As I mentioned above, even when those with addiction seek help, they are ambivalent about their addiction. Keep in mind, they have usually engaged in an addictive behavior, often daily, for years, so they must see this behavior as beneficial in some way. That's why it's important for me to understand what my patients' goals are rather than imposing my goals on them. This makes it possible to discover what *they* would like to accomplish for themselves, if and how they see their marijuana and other drug use as a problem in meeting their goals, and what would motivate them to change their behavior. If they have made it into my office for an evaluation, though, the problems associated with their use usually outweigh the perceived benefits, and my job is to help them see that. Doing this—having people recognize the problems associated with their use and articulate the need for change in their own words—is the key to helping them find the motivation to do the hard work required to stop using a substance that has given so much pleasure and appeared to help them cope with their problems in the past.[53] When we discover our own reasons and motivation for changing, we will be far more likely to accept help from others than if they lecture us or try to scare us by pushing a stack of scientific papers on the dangers of marijuana use onto our lap.

The second goal of an initial evaluation is to take a careful history. I often tell the psychiatry resident physicians I teach that the history they take may be the most comprehensive assessment the client ever receives. This is especially true in this era of medicine; doctors get to spend far too little time with patients. While marijuana use and other substance use should be the focus, it's important that a clinician gather information about a client's medical, psychiatric, and social histories. I want to know as much as I can about how they use.

- How many times a day do they use and when?

- Do they smoke or use a vaporizer or use marijuana in another way?

- How much marijuana do they use per week and how do they get it?

- Do they smoke alone or with friends?

- Have they tried to reduce or stop using marijuana before?

Why they smoke is an essential piece of information to learn, because it can shape the type of treatment I recommend. Patients who use marijuana daily or nearly every day will provide all of this information, and often considerably more, in great detail.

Other aspects of this part of the assessment often allow me to get a better sense as to why patients have been using marijuana in the way that they have. As discussed earlier in this book, a person's marijuana use can be connected to other psychiatric problems like anxiety and depression, so a detailed psychiatric history must include other psychiatric issues or even other psychiatric treatment, whether the patient has a history of physical or sexual abuse, and whether or not the person has contemplated suicide. Like other addictions, marijuana addiction does not typically exist in a vacuum. There are other important factors—psychiatric, medical, or social—that play a role in someone's use. In order to effectively treat someone, a clinician needs to be aware of all relevant issues and handle them appropriately. For example, marijuana withdrawal symptoms may worsen depressive symptoms, at least temporarily. If a client has attempted suicide before, then the clinician needs to monitor mood even more carefully than he or she would otherwise.

If other clinicians are involved in the patient's care, I need to know who they are and the client must give me written permission to contact them. Communication between clinicians increases the likelihood that important information, such as relevant parts of the patient's history and treatment recommendations, does not fall through the cracks. Clients' medical history and current medications may also be related to their marijuana use. For example, a client prescribed a low dose of an antidepressant for a long period of time may begin using marijuana more often in response to undertreated depression. The presence of other psychiatric or addiction problems in a patient's family is important information for the clinician to have.

Finally, clients' social history may provide important context to their use. Many times clients simply forget to mention important elements of their history that relate to their marijuana use, and a skilled clinician can be helpful in drawing out these elements. Alternatively, clients may not have carefully examined their lives to the degree that they understand how various aspects of their lives have influenced their marijuana use. This is why a careful, thoughtful assessment by a professional is crucial.

Another goal of an initial assessment is to build an alliance between the client and the clinician. This is more likely to happen if the clinician is an attentive, active listener who lets the client talk but asks questions to clarify when necessary. It is rare that someone is willing to listen to another for an hour in this age of texting and social media, so clients and their loved ones appreciate that this is a different experience than their everyday life. When a clinician asks the right questions to fill in important pieces of information, it serves another critical purpose: it lets the client know that the clinician is knowledgeable about marijuana. At the time of the initial assessment, clients may not be ready to make the necessary commitment to changing their marijuana use, but if they come away from that assessment knowing that a clinician cares about them and what they are doing, they will be more likely to feel comfortable reaching out when they are ready.

The final goal of an initial assessment to is make the correct treatment recommendations. I recommend some type of treatment almost always, except in the instance that someone had an isolated drug test that captured occasional recreational use. Even in that case, however, a careful evaluation must be conducted to make sure that the drug test is not the tip of the marijuana addiction iceberg. There are various elements to a comprehensive treatment plan for marijuana addiction, and not everybody needs all elements. This is where things get murky. There is no one-size-fits-all approach, and health care professionals should not expect clients or their families to know what types of treatment are either available or necessary.

From Assessment to Treatment

People who need help can be referred to a range of treatment options. Which option is appropriate for a particular individual depends on the severity of the person's problem, the type of co-occurring conditions (such as depression, anxiety, or other issues), and insurance coverage.[54] Below are some of the options. In chapters 9 and 10, I'll discuss some specific treatment practices that show promise for people addicted to marijuana.

The most intensive treatment options involve structured programs that usually last for weeks and involve individual and group counseling. Flying away to a ninety-day treatment program, as seen on the popular television show *Intervention* that chronicles addiction stories, may be feasible for some people with the financial means to do it, but this is not an option for most people. There are two basic types of residential programs, long-term and short-term. These programs generally address addiction to a variety of drugs and behaviors and are not solely geared toward treating marijuana addiction. Long-term programs generally are one to three months in duration while short-term, or acute, residential programs last two to four weeks. Long-term residential programs are not usually covered by insurance, and they typically cost anywhere from $6,000 to $60,000 a month. Insurance companies will pay for long-term residential programs if a person meets the following criteria:

- has tried less restrictive care multiple times without good outcomes

- has a medical condition that requires twenty-four-hour medical monitoring

- has extreme conditions in the home environment that would make it difficult for the person to maintain abstinence from marijuana at home

In both types of residential programs, residents will spend the bulk of their days in group therapy sessions with similar patients. As noted, long-term residential programs work well when there are significant stressors present in the home environment that would possibly impede the patient's progress in establishing abstinence from drugs at home. Some long-term residential programs offer assistance in helping patients assimilate back into the workforce. While some of these residential programs are excellent, the fact that most are not covered by insurance limits access considerably.

Less intensive treatment is also an option. For example, a partial hospital program is typically five hours a day for two weeks. Patients get mostly group therapy with individual therapy mixed in just as in a residential program, but they attend the program while living at home. If someone has tried less intensive treatment in the six months or so prior to a partial hospital admission, a private insurance company might cover this treatment.

The lowest level of a structured outpatient treatment program is an intensive outpatient program, which is typically three days a week for three hours at a time, for about two weeks, sometimes longer. The mix of group and individual therapy is usually the same as in a partial hospital program. This is the first level of structured treatment that private insurance companies will approve, and they often will require a patient to try intensive outpatient programs at least twice before approving a higher level of care.

Other types of treatment are recommended if a residential, partial hospital program, or intensive outpatient program is not necessary. These other types of treatment may also be recommended after a structured treatment program is complete. A behavioral intervention, such as talk therapy (individual or group), is often recommended, and we will cover these in chapter 9. Medications may also form a part of a treatment plan. If a patient has another psychiatric disorder such as depression or anxiety, a medication is often necessary. Medications may also be used to reduce marijuana use, and these are covered in chapter 10.

Group therapy is often helpful in substance use disorders. A group is a weekly meeting of the same individuals who convene to talk about problems they are having with a particular drug. If the patient has completed structured treatment programs and is now in individual psychotherapy, group therapy can be very helpful. Self-help groups like Alcoholics Anonymous, Narcotics Anonymous, or Marijuana Anonymous can be helpful supplemental treatments as well and are especially effective for many people requiring ongoing recovery management in preventing relapse. Finally, still other treatments may be useful if less structured care is necessary. Seminars or lectures can be helpful in some cases by educating patients about the addiction, and bibliotherapy (studying books relevant to the person's particular issues) can be useful in that way as well.

Summary

Marijuana problems are difficult to identify, but it is possible to detect these problems if one knows what to look for. Although a person who may have a problem may not always be observed using marijuana, there are signs and symptoms that may suggest a problem exists. If situations at work or school get worse over time, if the person gives up activities that he or she previously enjoyed, uses marijuana in dangerous situations, or uses despite obvious physical or psychological problems, there is likely a need for an evaluation by a professional to determine if the person is addicted to marijuana and may need help.

The initial approach for a clinician to engage someone who might have a marijuana addiction is crucial and may determine whether that person receives necessary treatment. There are four steps to do this: preparation, conversation, evaluation, and referral. Preparation is critical, as it is better to have an idea of what steps the clinician and client will take in order to take advantage of a window of opportunity. It's most effective when clinicians use nonjudgmental conversation and are clear in stating that they think a client may have a problem and they want to assist that client in getting help.

The initial referral usually is to a professional who can perform an evaluation. A thorough initial evaluation is necessary to open the door to the appropriate level of care for a given individual's problem. There are many levels of treatment available, from residential programs, which the person attends for up to three months, to a variety of outpatient treatment options from individual therapy to group therapy to self-directed treatments like Marijuana Anonymous and seminars.

9

Behavioral Interventions as Treatment for Marijuana Addiction

Systematic research on treating marijuana addiction began with the evaluation of behavioral interventions in the 1980s. Behavioral interventions, or "talk therapies," can help people make significant reductions in their marijuana smoking. There are at least two important reasons for this. One is that very few people have ever thought about or examined their addiction issues in great detail. This means thinking, for more than just a few minutes at a time, about their marijuana use and how it impacts their lives. Second, most people have never worked with a therapist before. Having an objective person help you examine your life can be extremely helpful. The therapist listens and asks questions that help you understand why you are having problems and what you can do to correct these problems.*

Understanding Behavioral Interventions

There are many types of behavioral interventions, or talk therapies, available to treat marijuana addiction. Motivational

---

*In this chapter, I review the recent scientific literature on behavioral interventions for marijuana addiction. For more detailed reviews of each of these methods, please see the paper I published in 2014 with Dr. Aaron Bobb in *Current Treatment Options in Psychiatry* entitled "Behavioral Interventions and Pharmacotherapies for Cannabis Use Disorder."

interviewing (MI), cognitive behavioral therapy (CBT), motivational enhancement therapy (MET), contingency management (CM), and multidimensional family therapy (MDFT) have been shown to be effective. Self-help peer support groups like Alcoholics Anonymous, Narcotics Anonymous, and Marijuana Anonymous have also proven helpful in treating marijuana addiction and are often combined with talk therapies—especially in providing recovery support over time. One interesting result of these studies is that there are not significant differences between results from one talk therapy to another. This means that it does not matter so much what kind of therapy is used; rather, the important thing is that the person receives therapy from someone with whom they can establish a trusting relationship. The studies of these therapies typically show a 20 to 60 percent reduction in marijuana use after short-term (usually less than three months) therapy. Marijuana use often slowly increases again once the therapy is stopped. Other studies have shown that ongoing attendance in peer support groups can help people sustain abstinence or reduced use for a longer period of time. This level of reduction, or successful outcome, compares favorably with the outcomes of treatments for other addictions.

Stephen

Stephen is a twenty-five-year-old contractor with no previous psychiatric history who applied for one of the clinical trials I direct. Stephen smoked marijuana four to five times per day and had done so for the past four years. He also drank two to eight beers five nights a week (usually two nights with around four to five beers a night), but he noted that he used to drink more before he started using marijuana regularly. When he drank more in the past, he was smoking marijuana once or twice a week. He said that he preferred the way he felt after smoking marijuana to when he was hung over (what he called "the Irish

Flu"). He had one young son and another child with his fiancée was on the way, and he no longer wanted to spend money on marijuana. His marijuana use had become more of an issue in his relationship, as his fiancée did not want him to smoke around the children and she did not see regular marijuana use as something that accomplished, married people should do. Aside from that, Stephen also knew that "it isn't healthy for me."

Stephen was accepted into the clinical trial and received ten weeks of cognitive behavioral therapy (CBT) aimed at helping him address the thoughts, feelings, and behaviors that contributed to his daily smoking habit. We looked carefully at the specific times during the day that he smoked and what his feelings were at these times. Over the course of ten weeks, Stephen was able to reduce his smoking from four to five times daily to one to two times a week. He also reduced his drinking to once or twice a week, typically three to four beers a night.

It is important to point out that many who receive therapy do not completely stop using marijuana, although they may want to. However, while the goal of treatment is abstinence—zero use of marijuana—patients who are unable to completely stop using marijuana can still have clinically significant reductions in use. "Clinically significant" means that the reductions result in improvements in the important areas of their lives that led them into treatment in the first place, usually work, school, or relationships. For example, if Stephen, the contractor, is using marijuana four to five times a day, every day, at the start of treatment, and he is able to reduce his use to twice a week (while also cutting back on his drinking), that is a clinically significant reduction. This level of reduction should result in improvements in Stephen's work performance. Therefore, treatment can still be considered successful even if the patient is not able to completely stop using marijuana.

Motivational interviewing

Motivational interviewing is about helping people change. It is a style of communication developed by Dr. William Miller and Dr. Stephen Rollnick that addresses ambivalence. "Ambivalence" means that clients know deep down that they need help for a problem, but their readiness to engage in the therapeutic process waxes and wanes. This is a feeling reported by many people with addictions. They may be highly motivated for treatment on one day and willing to do whatever it takes to stop using, but the next day they are not so motivated, for a variety of reasons. Motivational interviewing was designed with ambivalence in mind, and it is a conversational, collaborative, goal-oriented style of communication that aims to address ambivalence while increasing motivation for change. The clinician must be skilled to appreciate the difference between "change talk"—words from the client that indicate that he or she is indeed considering making an effort to stop using—and "sustain talk"—words from the patient signifying that he or she is considering continuing use. I use MI as a part of my initial evaluation, in conjunction with the cognitive behavioral therapy that I do with patients, and even at other times during a treatment if necessary.

Elise

Elise is a seventeen-year-old high school junior with a past medical history of depression whose parents brought her to see me after she was asked to leave a boarding school in the region. She first smoked marijuana as a freshman, but started to smoke regularly during her sophomore year because "all of my friends did it." Her grades dipped from As and B-pluses as a freshman to B-pluses and Bs. She was caught with marijuana toward the end of her sophomore year and her parents sent her to a local psychiatrist who was recommended to them.

Elise was started on an antidepressant and saw the psychiatrist monthly throughout the summer before returning to boarding school. Unfortunately, a month into her junior year she was caught again with marijuana in her room and was expelled, per school policy.

She saw me for her initial evaluation as she was about to begin attending a local private day school in the middle of the fall semester. She did not think that her smoking "was a big deal," but she described ongoing, near-daily anxiety about her academic performance; she was especially concerned about how getting expelled would affect her chances of getting into the colleges she was about to apply to. This concern was the primary motivation for her to continue to see me for a combination of motivational interviewing and cognitive behavioral therapy. Her parents admitted that they were not initially very worried about her use, but they were alarmed now, and this led them to do some more digging about marijuana addiction prior to contacting me.

In the first six weeks of treatment, she smoked marijuana twice, but she became increasingly invested in the work we were doing. Our CBT focused on the feelings around her marijuana use—mostly anxiety—and we discussed healthier ways to manage these feelings aside from smoking. She performed well academically and seemed to enjoy living at home while attending school.

I used MI in my early sessions with Elise in an effort to have her articulate why she wanted to try to stop using marijuana. This is an example of meeting people where they are and listening carefully to assess their readiness to make a significant effort at stopping. This is done with the understanding that clients have a better chance of being successful if they articulate and understand why they are trying to stop, as opposed to the clinician telling them why they should stop. The process can be powerful—the client and the therapist working together to frame the client's motivation for change—and a great endorsement for someone using therapy to address marijuana use in general. A skilled professional can help clients who are unable to control their use on their own see things they might not otherwise see and, as a result, they can make strides toward a healthy lifestyle that they might not have otherwise made.

Motivational enhancement therapy

Motivational enhancement therapy (MET) is based on the principles of MI and typically entails one to four therapy sessions. The difference between MI and MET is that MI is a therapeutic style that can be incorporated into various treatment approaches, while MET is a specific application of MI. As noted, I use MI at various times during a treatment if necessary. MET has been studied in an effort to develop shorter treatment programs that are more likely to be used than long psychotherapy programs. In a famous study called Project MATCH, engaging clients in four sessions of MET was found to be as effective as using twelve sessions of CBT or Twelve Step Facilitation Therapy (based on the use of Alcoholics Anonymous) as a treatment for alcohol addiction.[55]

Cognitive behavioral therapy

As we noted earlier, cognitive behavioral therapy centers around thoughts, feelings, and actions. It can be used for a variety of psychiatric disorders including addiction. CBT aims to teach patients skills and coping strategies to use when confronted with the challenges of trying to stop using marijuana and to stay away from it when stopped. The therapist teaches the client to recognize triggers that might lead to use and cravings to use. Homework is often given for additional help in developing CBT skills. CBT is also useful in allowing patients an opportunity to strategize about high-risk situations they may face. Thinking about these situations in advance, as opposed to being surprised when faced with a high-risk event, reduces the likelihood that the client will make an impulsive decision to use. The therapist and the client role-play prior to such high-risk situations as well, affording the patient a chance to practice skills of drug refusal, for example.

I used a combination of MI and CBT with both Stephen and Elise, employing MI mostly in the first couple of sessions to help frame their motivation to stop using marijuana. Like most people addicted to marijuana, Elise was ambivalent about stopping, in part because she saw so many of her friends using in the same way that she was and they had not suffered consequences as she had. She was motivated, however, to keep her hopes of attending a few colleges in particular alive, and this led her to work hard in therapy and on her own to change her use of marijuana. Most young people are like Elise: they are not motivated by data from research studies; they are motivated by tangible things—her college career in this case. It is important that young people are aware of the science of marijuana so they know what the facts are, but they are more likely to make an effort to change in order to get something they want or to avoid losing something than because there are studies that show marijuana negatively affects their cognitive abilities.

Stephen was motivated by more practical matters. He thought that he was spending too much money on marijuana. While marijuana is not the most expensive drug that is abused, regular marijuana use is cost prohibitive for many people. He also felt that his marijuana use may have been affecting his work as a contractor. He had a sense that smoking multiple times a day, including before work, was probably not healthy for him. He had previously understood that being hung over from alcohol was not good for his work performance, and he began to wonder if his marijuana use was also adversely affecting his work.

CBT can be labor intensive and it is not easy to do for either the clinician or client, but it works. When I am doing CBT with clients to help them stop using marijuana, I want to know about every instance during the day that they typically use. I ask them why they think they smoke at those particular times and what benefit they think they are getting. These answers change for different parts of the day. A regular user might smoke first thing in the morning to lessen feelings of anxiety or to feel "normal" enough to face the day. Often marijuana users describe smoking after work as a reward in the same way that others might describe having an alcoholic drink when they get home. Finally, marijuana users might feel the need to smoke before going to bed in order to have a chance of getting a good night's sleep. Each of these instances requires a different conversation and a different approach, but all of them must be addressed successfully if the person is going to be able to stop using marijuana.

Contingency management

Contingency management (CM) is a behavioral intervention based on rewarding targeted behaviors. Clients are given a reward, such as a voucher for an item or money, for a urine test that is free of any substances, for example. CM relies on "operant conditioning," the process by which behaviors are modified based on rewards or punishments. In CM for substance use disorders, patients may receive rewards for drug-free urine drug screens, attending treatment, or doing CBT homework.

With CM, punishment can occur when bad behaviors happen by reducing opportunity to earn rewards or diminishing the value of rewards earned. The value of the reward typically increases each time the patient achieves the desired outcome;

when a client engages in undesired behavior, he or she is "punished," meaning that the reward reverts back to the original value. CM has also been added to other combinations of talk therapy to boost outcomes. Dr. Kathleen Carroll and her colleagues from Yale, for example, showed in a study of adolescents with marijuana addiction that adding CM to a combination of MET plus CBT or a more generic drug counseling resulted in significantly longer periods of abstinence from marijuana as well as significantly more marijuana-free urine drug screens.[56]

CM has been shown to be effective for a variety of disorders, including marijuana addiction, although there are concerns about it in health care. Some see the rewards as payment and do not think that people should be paid for doing things they should already be motivated to do, like taking care of themselves. Another major concern about CM is how to pay for it. It is difficult already to fund treatment programs, and funding sources often are hesitant to add additional funds to be used for rewards on top of the usual costs of treatment such as staff salaries.

Multidimensional family therapy

Multidimensional family therapy (MDFT) is a type of talk therapy for adolescents and their parents. The clinician meets with both the adolescent and his or her parents individually and together. In addition to addressing drug use and the development of coping skills related to addiction, family issues are addressed. Interpersonal issues within the family, family functioning, parenting skills, and limit setting are worked on in MDFT. A study by Dr. Howard Liddle and colleagues from the University of Miami comparing MDFT with CBT in adolescents with marijuana addiction showed that participants treated with either treatment were able to significantly reduce their marijuana use and there was no significant difference in outcomes from MDFT or CBT.[57]

Self-help group attendance

Self-help, or peer support, group meetings are important behavioral interventions as well. Self-help group meetings should not take the place of individual talk therapy or medication, but they are an important piece of the puzzle. I find them very useful in adding structure to a patient's week and I generally recommend that patients try to attend two to three self-help meetings each week, although some go every day and some people with sustained abstinence never go to meetings anymore. Most people have heard of Alcoholics Anonymous (AA), a mutual aid fellowship using the Twelve Step model of recovery where those with a history of alcohol addiction try to maintain sobriety in an atmosphere of mutual support. AA, like other Twelve Step support groups, differs from talk therapy groups in that there is no "cross-talk" and support is provided by listening and example. There is a spiritual component in Twelve Step programs whereby participants acknowledge their inability to control their use on their own and the need for a higher power (such as a God of the person's understanding, nature, or the group itself) that is greater than the individual. Narcotics Anonymous (NA) is similar to AA except that it addresses the use of narcotics like opioids and other drugs more than it addresses alcohol use. As the name implies, Marijuana Anonymous (MA) groups provide support specifically for people addicted to marijuana. My clients who have attended these meetings report that it is especially helpful to talk about their problems with others who understand the intricacies of having marijuana addiction in a society where many people do not believe you can be addicted to this drug. If an MA group isn't available, either AA or NA can provide a place to get support for addiction to any drug since there are so many common issues among all addicts. AA states specifically that it is for recovery from alcoholism, but many members have multiple addictions and find it helpful to address these common issues instead of focusing on their drug of choice.

Self-management and recovery training (SMART) is a non-Twelve Step group that relies on rational thinking similar to the talk therapy techniques we've discussed to address addiction. Some people find that the spiritual component to AA or NA does not resonate with them and often prefer SMART recovery meetings.

My Approach to Behavioral Interventions in Early Treatment

While my approach may not be exactly what you might find in working with a therapist to deal with your marijuana use problems, I'll describe it here to give an example of how some of the behavioral therapies we've just covered might look in application. In many cases where marijuana addiction appears to be the core issue, I will use a combination of motivational interviewing and cognitive behavioral therapy during early treatment. Usually I will see a person for up to four meetings, what might be referred to as "readiness" sessions, before we decide whether or not to continue treatment, make a referral to another clinician, or that the person is not ready for additional treatment at this point.

Along with acknowledging that there are aspects of marijuana use that clients enjoy, it is important to address the grief that comes with being forced to accept the reality that you need to stop doing something that you enjoy. This is a special challenge for young people. They undoubtedly have friends who can seemingly use whatever drugs they wish on a particular evening and then go about their business the next day with no trouble at all. I point out to clients who are sitting across from me for an evaluation that, for a variety of reasons, including their genetics, if they are addicted to marijuana, they are not able to use drugs with reckless abandon as their friends might. This is a crushing realization for many young people, and it is hard to deal with. I believe it is important to address this grief head-on and have found that doing so makes it more likely that clients will acknowledge their frustration and sadness about being in a position where it is recommended that they stop using marijuana. Being aware of these feelings puts the patient in a better position to manage these feelings over time rather than saying "F--- it" and continuing to use.

Once clients are able to see that treatment would be useful to them, I prefer to start talk therapy on a weekly basis. Weekly is important; fifty minutes is a relatively small investment to make with a tremendous potential return. An experienced psychiatrist once explained to me that fifty minutes spent in meaningful therapy can affect the rest of the week in a positive fashion. I find that if a client comes less frequently than weekly, precious minutes are spent at the beginning of each session filling in the therapist on what the client has been up to since the last session. It is easy to spend a quarter of the session that way, and that is not the best use of the session.

Once we agree that the patient would benefit from weekly psychotherapy and we agree to work together, I usually prefer to use CBT to explore the specific instances in which the person typically uses marijuana and the thoughts, feelings, and behaviors involved in these instances. The client and I then lay out his or her pattern of marijuana use in great detail— number of times per day, when during the day, alone or not, the benefits of using, and so on. The client will likely describe several discrete instances each day that he or she uses marijuana, and these instances will be connected to different situations and feelings.

In addition, I discourage the use of other addictive substances while they are in treatment. The relationship between multiple addictive substances is a controversial one among those who treat people with addiction. Some feel that use of one addictive substance both increases the likelihood that someone will use other addictive substances and can worsen treatment outcomes if a person is in treatment for addiction to another substance. Marijuana is a classic example of this debate. If someone is in treatment for opioid addiction, for example, then many clinicians feel that marijuana use may open the door to relapse into opioid addiction. Another outstanding clinician I know has run many opioid addiction treatment programs, and he feels that it is not worth the effort and cost to test for marijuana use among those with opioid addiction. The research on these issues is inconclusive. In a 2012 study that I published, I asked whether marijuana use worsens treatment outcomes for patients in treatment for opioid addiction. It did not in my study, but studies have come out on both sides of this issue.[58] Although my own study did not show an adverse effect from marijuana use among people with opioid addiction, I still encourage my patients to avoid use of all addictive substances when in treatment.

I often use CBT techniques to help clients understand how behaviors result from certain situations, using this formula:

Situation > > **Thoughts** > > **Feelings** > > **Behaviors**

For example, Stephen feels worried about his relationship with his fiancée not going as well as he would like and he smokes marijuana. The difficulty in the relationship is the situation. Stephen's thought about the situation might be "There is nothing I can do to make this better." His feelings about the difficult situation might be helplessness, hopelessness, and depressed mood. Smoking marijuana is the behavior. The clinician would have Stephen draw out this chain and see how one of the links in the chain affects the others. It is important to try to help the client understand that a situation does not cause a behavior; you make a choice about how you are going to respond to a given situation. In this case, it is easy to see how Stephen might choose to have a positive thought about the situation as opposed to the negative thought described above. "I am going to do whatever I can to make this better" is a positive, proactive thought that in turn makes it more likely that Stephen will feel in control, hopeful, and calm about his chances of making things better. This is not easy work to do in a session, and few people want to take on homework assignments from their therapist, but this is precisely the kind of exercise that makes CBT so effective.

Relapse prevention is another piece to the effectiveness of CBT. Each week in CBT, we review high-risk situations that the client has experienced as well as ones that may arise before our next session. If a party at which many people will be smoking marijuana is on the horizon, for example, it is useful to discuss what that may be like and how clients might handle things if they are offered marijuana or how they would handle the feeling that they should leave. Clients are more likely to respond appropriately to such situations if they are not surprised by them. Thinking about situations beforehand, and possibly even role-playing various situations, helps clients plan to avoid relapse.

I have found that CBT aimed at reducing substance abuse can be delivered effectively in approximately ten sessions. If clients are motivated to make a change and work hard during the sessions and on their homework assignments, it is likely that they will be able to make a meaningful reduction in their use during the ten-week treatment.

Summary

Behavioral interventions can be effective treatments for marijuana addiction. Used alone or alongside other treatments, these interventions center around a therapist or a group helping clients examine their marijuana use and situations related to it. There are many different types of behavioral interventions that can be part of a successful treatment; data seems to point to the duration and intensity of the intervention as being more important than the structure of the treatment itself to a large degree. Behavioral interventions are a staple in both my private practice and my clinical trials. In my private practice, I use motivational interviewing techniques in the early portion of treatment to help clients articulate why they think they should change their marijuana use. I also use cognitive behavioral therapy, a type of therapy that focuses on the thoughts, feelings, and behaviors associated with marijuana use. If patients are motivated to change their marijuana use and to work hard to achieve this both during a therapy session and outside of it, behavioral interventions can help people achieve significant reductions in their marijuana use.

10

Using Medications to Treat Marijuana Addiction

Despite the alarming numbers of Americans addicted to marijuana—approximately 2.7 million—and the trends that suggest those numbers are increasing, there are no FDA-approved medications for the treatment of marijuana addiction. Research into the development of such medications started around the year 2000. Right now, there are research groups at prominent universities, including our research group at McLean/Harvard, working feverishly to develop medications that may help people change their marijuana use habits.

Brian

Brian was a twenty-seven-year-old insurance salesman with a past medical history of anxiety and marijuana addiction who called me because he wanted to stop using marijuana. He was smoking four to five times a day and had been using marijuana in this manner for six years. He had tried to stop on his own and had failed, aside from brief periods when he was out of the country. He was not sure if his smoking was affecting his performance at work, but he was convinced that his smoking was hindering his relationship with women. "They can't believe how much I smoke and I think it ends up turning them off," he confided.

He was ambivalent about coming in every week to do cognitive behavioral therapy, but he was willing to try it. After a few
weeks, he noted that he was working hard to reduce his use of
marijuana and was probably smoking about three times a day.
He said it was harder than he had planned and he wondered
if there were medications that might help. He had been prescribed an antidepressant before he came to see me and was
still taking it. We discussed medications that could be used
off-label to help him stop using marijuana, and I prescribed him
300 milligrams of gabapentin three times daily.

After another month of CBT and medication, he reported
that he felt better about his use, which had dropped to about
twice daily three to four times a week. At that point, I referred
Brian at his request to another therapist with an office closer to
his place of employment.

There are several different approaches that can be taken
to develop medications for marijuana addiction such as I prescribed for Brian. In this chapter, I will review the approaches,
review some of the common medications that have been studied, and look at the use of medication to treat co-occurring
disorders that people with marijuana use disorders often have.
Let's begin by discussing what it means to see—and treat—
marijuana addiction as a chronic disease.*

Treating a Chronic Disease

In order to understand how medications might work as treatments for marijuana addiction, it's helpful to think of the addiction as a chronic medical illness. A chronic illness is a disease

---

*For more detailed reviews of many of these medications, please see the paper I
published in 2014 with Dr. Aaron Bobb in *Current Treatment Options in Psychiatry* entitled "Behavioral Interventions and Pharmacotherapies for Cannabis Use
Disorder."

or disorder that usually progresses slowly and lasts a long time (years). The uncomfortable symptoms can be continuous or may come and go. Medical problems like asthma, diabetes, and high blood pressure are all examples of chronic illnesses. Addiction is also a chronic illness, usually taking some years to develop, lasting many years, and occurring either continuously or in episodes (times of sobriety or low use followed by times of uncontrolled high use).

Addiction still bears a stigma in the United States, though, and people suffering from addiction are often looked down upon. Some feel that people with addiction have flawed morals, as though they have consciously chosen to develop addiction. As we saw in chapter 4, however, many factors play a role in addiction, including genetics. Studies have shown that genetics play as much a role in addiction as they do in asthma, diabetes, and high blood pressure. Just as marijuana shares many important characteristics with other drugs we accept as addictive, addiction shares many important characteristics with other chronic medical illnesses that afflict millions of Americans.

Most chronic illnesses can't be cured. They require some form of ongoing treatment or management. Sometimes this means medication, but it can also mean lifestyle changes. For example, people with diabetes or high blood pressure can manage their diseases by combining the right medications, proper diet, and adequate exercise. People with asthma may use inhalers daily and also control their exposure to items known to trigger their asthma, such as cats or mold.

Medications don't cure asthma, diabetes, and high blood pressure, and they won't cure addiction, either. But just as people take medications to effectively manage these chronic medical illnesses, the goal is to develop medications for addiction that can work the same way. Buprenorphine, a medication used to treat addiction to opioid drugs (prescription painkillers like oxycodone, hydrocodone, and fentanyl and illegal drugs like heroin and opium), is an example of a successful addiction medication.

When a person has a chronic illness, the rigors of maintaining health can be frustrating. People with diabetes, for instance, can take a medication or a combination of medications and function well in all areas of their lives. But they may sometimes lose strict control of their blood sugars and need to be hospitalized for a brief period in order to get things back under control. The same is true for patients with opioid addiction who take buprenorphine. They can function well in their lives while taking the medication, but there may be times when they lose control of their addiction temporarily and require a brief hospitalization.

Unfortunately, the stigma against addiction keeps many people from making an all-out effort at using addiction medications like buprenorphine to gain control of their lives. Another reason that people with addiction refuse to take an addiction medication is peer pressure. Many people are able to control an addiction without the use of a medication, relying primarily on some form of treatment, a self-help group, or both. Some who did not require medications to become drug-free scoff at the need for medication to establish abstinence. Others with addiction become keenly aware of the instances where buprenorphine is misused or abused itself. Many patients with opioid addiction so severe that they had already suffered major losses in school, work, or relationships have flatly refused to consider taking a medication aimed at helping them regain function in their lives. "I don't want to trade one drug addiction for another," they say. Of course, I have never heard a patient say that they were addicted to insulin or their blood pressure medication. This illustrates why it is so important to try to educate the public that addiction is a chronic medical illness.

Promising Medications

Some medications for addiction use what are called "antagonist" drugs. These are compounds that block the effect of the addictive substance. Other compounds called "agonist" medications provide some effects similar to the drug of abuse, but not as strong. Some studies that have been done or are ongoing use agonist medications to help people reduce their use. For example, buprenorphine and methadone are both agonists that help with opioid addiction. The nicotine patch contains an agonist that helps for tobacco cigarette smoking cessation.

It's logical to ask, what could possibly be helpful about agonists, since they produce effects similar to those of the drug a person is trying to quit? Isn't it more logical to use an antagonist—a drug that blocks the effect?

The reason that agonists may be helpful has to do, in part, with the overwhelming discomfort caused by withdrawal symptoms. In chapter 5 we saw that those who use marijuana daily or nearly every day can have powerful and unpleasant withdrawal symptoms if they try to stop smoking abruptly. The symptoms are so strong that the user feels that quitting is worse than continuing, at least in the short term, and the withdrawal symptoms often lead to relapse. Agonist drugs can help a person by reducing withdrawal, which helps break the powerful urge to use again. Agonist medications for marijuana addiction are being studied in clinical trials in an effort to reduce or eliminate some of the withdrawal symptoms associated with stopping marijuana use.

Some of the medications under review for possible use in treating marijuana addiction include the cannabinoid agonists dronabinol, nabiximols, and nabilone; N-acetylcysteine, an over-the-counter supplement that has been used as an antidote for Tylenol overdoses; gabapentin (brand name Neurontin), which has been used to treat seizure disorders and has also seen some success in reducing marijuana use in clinical trials; and buspirone, an anti-anxiety medication that has shown modest success in a trial study with marijuana addicts. These and various other medications that have been studied in clinical trials are described in more detail in appendix A.

Co-occurring Disorders and Medications

People who are addicted to marijuana are likely to have other psychiatric problems. Therefore, successful treatment must also address other conditions that occur along with the marijuana addiction, including anxiety, depression, insomnia, and attention-deficit hyperactivity disorder (ADHD). This underscores the importance of a thorough evaluation by a skilled clinician at the outset of treatment. The clinician must carefully probe for other problems that the patient may not even be aware of. Unfortunately, some clinicians are not skilled in addressing multiple issues. Some become such specialists in treating particular disorders that they do not ask the right questions about other problems a person might have.

Co-occurring psychiatric problems are usually best addressed with both talk therapy and medications. While the "chicken and the egg" debate can be had over the relationship between anxiety, depression, and marijuana addiction, it is clear that these problems tend to occur together. Patients cannot reasonably be expected to do well if they have depression and marijuana addiction, for example, and only one of these issues is being addressed in treatment. Treating anxiety or depression with medications successfully can put patients in a better position to make a change in their marijuana use. In these cases, I like to start medication at the same time we are trying to address marijuana use. There is no need to wait to treat co-occurring problems—multiple problems can be treated at once, just as Brian continued with his antidepressant in the earlier case example. Antidepressants can be used to treat both depression and anxiety. If the person has an anxiety disorder, I may prescribe a nonaddictive medication for anxiety as well.

Insomnia and ADHD are other medical problems that often co-occur in patients with marijuana addiction. It is hard to imagine that anyone would be able to do something as difficult as stopping marijuana use if he or she has trouble sleeping. In addition, clients may report that their last marijuana smoking session of the evening is aimed at helping them get to sleep. In these cases, a time-limited trial of a nonaddictive medication for insomnia may make sense. Treating patients with marijuana addiction in addition to ADHD is trickier because the first-line medications for ADHD are stimulants like Ritalin and Adderall, which are addictive in their own right. There are nonaddictive medications for ADHD available, such as atomoxetine and the antidepressant bupropion. If the patient lives with a family member who can be in charge of storing the stimulant and responsible for giving it to the patient every day, I would consider prescribing a stimulant, simply because in my experience, they are considerably more effective for treating ADHD than nonaddictive medications for ADHD.

Medications for marijuana addiction should be a part of a comprehensive treatment plan. Such a plan includes a behavioral intervention (such as CBT), medications to treat co-occurring disorders such as anxiety or depression, and self-help groups like Marijuana Anonymous. If most of these elements are in place, I will discuss with patients the possibility of using a medication as an aid to the current treatment plan, the evidence supporting the use of such medications, symptoms that particular patients may have in relation to their marijuana use, and possible side effects. While any other medications they might need and self-help are useful to have in place when starting a medication, the lack of talk therapy is the only element that would keep me from prescribing a medication for marijuana addiction right away. If the patient envisions the medication being the entire treatment plan, the plan is unlikely to be successful.

It's shortsighted to think that a bottle of medication alone is going to help you manage a problem as complex as marijuana addiction. I have used both gabapentin and N-acetylcysteine off-label in my private practice, as they have the strongest evidence thus far. While I remain excited about the possibilities of cannabinoid agonists like dronabinol and nabilone, the lack of strong data thus far and the more significant potential side effects of these medications have kept me from utilizing them in my private practice.

Summary
Even though approximately 2.7 million Americans are addicted to marijuana, there are no FDA-approved medications for marijuana addiction. Addiction is a chronic medical illness like asthma, diabetes, or high blood pressure, so it is reasonable to expect that medications would be helpful in treating marijuana addiction. Medications like dronabinol, nabiximols, nabilone, N-acetylcysteine, gabapentin, and buspirone have shown promise as treatments for marijuana addiction, and some of these medications can be considered by doctors as possible aids to a comprehensive treatment plan. These and other medications continue to be studied in randomized controlled trials in an effort to develop an effective, and perhaps FDA-approved, medication for marijuana addiction. People with marijuana addiction often have other problems like depression, anxiety, insomnia, and ADHD, and these problems can be treated with medications while simultaneously addressing marijuana addiction with medications, behavioral interventions, or a combination of these.

11

The Effect of Marijuana Addiction on Loved Ones

During the course of this book, we have covered all of the important aspects of marijuana. We have investigated the pharmacology, the statistics, the popular myths, and the changing public policies related to marijuana. Unlike most other books on the subject of marijuana, we have covered the treatment of marijuana in great detail, from the identification of someone with a marijuana use disorder, to what an initial evaluation of such a problem looks like, to treatment of marijuana addiction with both behavioral interventions and medications. In this chapter, we turn our attention toward the other people who are most significantly affected by marijuana use: the loved ones of the person who is using.

Marijuana has the potential to affect many more people than just the person who uses. This is especially true if occasional marijuana use progresses to marijuana addiction. Family and friends are often forced to deal with many intertwined aspects of addiction when their loved one begins to lose control over their marijuana use. Not only are addiction and the many problems that accompany it challenging to confront, but the timing of these problems also adds to the difficulty of these situations. Just as there is never a good time for your car to break down, there is never a good time for someone's addiction to progress to the point where immediate help is needed. Having a loved one in the midst of a battle with addiction can be incredibly exhausting and overwhelming. Families often do not know where to turn.

That is the point of this chapter. Those of you seeking help or trying to learn about marijuana because you suspect someone you care about may have a problem with it may find comfort in knowing that there are millions of other people who share your experiences. It is an unenviable position to be in—to realize that someone you love has an addiction to marijuana, a drug that so many people feel is not addictive. Once that realization is made, however, friends and family members need to know what to do, both for the person with the problem and for themselves.

Adult Addiction

Doria's case illustrates common ways in which marijuana addiction in adults can affect their family.

Doria

Doria is a twenty-five-year-old single mother who has smoked marijuana daily for most of the past nine years. She smokes three to four times a day; first in the morning within fifteen minutes of waking up, a couple of other times during the day, including her lunch break at work as an actuary, and once in the evening. She almost always smokes by herself; she says that it relaxes her and makes everything "more fun and enjoyable." She thinks that her marijuana use has made her somewhat less productive at work, but she has progressed just fine to this point, passing the exams that are required periodically. The biggest drawback she sees to her smoking is that it may have hindered her recent attempts at dating. She noted that men she has dated are surprised when they figure out how much she smokes and, although no one has explicitly stated this as a reason for ending the relationship, she has had difficulty extending relationships beyond more than a few weeks.

Her parents originally called to set up the evaluation with me because they were worried that Doria's marijuana use was escalating. They said that they sat idly by for years hoping that Doria would outgrow her marijuana use. Her parents frequently offered to babysit Doria's three-year-old son, and Doria would take them up on these offers. However, she had begun to call them more frequently for babysitting help, sometimes on short notice, and this was taking its toll on her parents. She had tried a few times to stop using marijuana on her own and was able to stop for most of her pregnancy. But she admitted now that she was not overly motivated to stop using, despite her parents' concerns about how her marijuana use was affecting her relationship with her son, her parents, and her career potential.

Her parents came to the consultation as well, and Doria said it would be fine for them to join us for the last thirty minutes or so. The discussion became heated very quickly at this point; Doria and her parents argued about how much Doria had her marijuana use under control. Her parents expressed far more concern about it than she did. She attempted to assure them that she had control of her smoking and that her job was secure. She also pointed out that their eagerness to see their grandson actually made it harder for her to become motivated to take the necessary steps to stop smoking marijuana daily.

Doria's case is typical of many people who are not sure if they are addicted to marijuana. She continues to function at a reasonably high level, especially at work where she has continued to be productive and is moving along an appropriate career trajectory. While she suspects that she could be even more productive at work if she did not smoke several times a day, that fact does not motivate her to attempt to change her smoking. It is the possible impact that her marijuana use is having on her social life that motivates her more than anything else. She has not been in a meaningful romantic relationship for several years and wants badly to rectify this situation, and has begun to wonder if her marijuana use might be part of the problem.

While Doria has continued to use marijuana regularly for years and is still trying to decide how harmful it has been for her, her use affects several of her family members. Her parents are shouldering a heavy load; they are worried about their daughter losing her job and they are spending more time babysitting Doria's three-year-old son than they anticipated. Trying to keep up with a three-year-old is hard work, but having to do it on nights when you were not planning to is another story altogether. In the "no good deed goes unpunished" category, Doria actually pointed the finger at them, saying that they had hindered her recovery process in part because they were so responsive to her pleas for help. This is a classic example of how those struggling with addiction find it easier to blame others for their problems than to take responsibility themselves.

Doria's parents, like many loved ones of people addicted to marijuana, often feel bad about not having figured things out more quickly. They wonder how things might have been different if they had acted sooner. But they don't have to feel bad about being duped for so long, because those with addiction problems are very skilled at hiding their habits. Keep in mind, addicts are able to fool many people in their lives—spouses, family, friends, co-workers, even their doctors. In hindsight, many people say that the signs were there with their loved ones, but it is very difficult to detect such problems in real time, especially if you have not had previous experience with addiction. Another issue that may delay the detection of a marijuana problem is the use of marijuana by other friends and family. As discussed in chapter 2, marijuana use is on the rise, making it hard to point at someone's use and call it a problem when so many other adults are using as well.

There are other reasons family members wait before acting on a possible marijuana addiction. They may be afraid of the unpleasant confrontation that might occur. People with addiction usually don't want to be exposed and they, therefore, can be quite nasty should they choose to be. Family members may fear costing their loved one a job or a relationship if they bring attention to the addiction problem. They may not know how to broach the topic. They may fear that bringing up the topic of addiction might end up in a discussion of their own shortcomings, whether addiction-related or otherwise. Or they might hope that, if they do nothing, the problem might simply just go away.

Doria's marijuana use also affects her relationship with her young son. But it is harder to assess these effects than it is to assess the effects of her use on the relationship with her parents. Doria's need to call on her parents for emergency babysitting would seem to represent a choice to spend time away from her son, time that might be spent in the pursuit of marijuana or use of it. With Doria smoking marijuana multiple times a day, we must ask whether she is taking the best care of her son while under the influence of marijuana. Whether her marijuana use compromises her ability to care for her son is debatable without examining blood levels of THC to determine her level of impairment, but even if marijuana only makes her less likely to fully engage in play with her son, then that is a negative outcome from her use.

Marijuana addiction can affect spouses and close friends as well. A typical clinical scenario involves a relationship in which people have used marijuana, often together, for years. A conflict arises when someone, a spouse or a close friend, decides that regular marijuana use is not conducive to achieving the goals he or she aspires to. Friends typically grow apart in such instances. Romantic relationships, because they are more intense, are stickier when such a conflict occurs. Spouses may make it clear that they no longer plan to use marijuana in the manner they did before and that they hope their partner will do the same. An ultimatum may follow—*quit using marijuana or we are done.* I don't recommend using ultimatums if your goal is to get someone to quit, unless you're prepared to follow through with the consequence you've set; if users are truly addicted, they are likely to choose their drug over most other things, including a relationship.

Adolescent Addiction

Bobby's case illustrates how a young person's marijuana use can adversely affect an entire family.

Bobby

Bobby is a seventeen-year-old high school junior referred to me for an evaluation after his parents caught him smoking marijuana in their house for the third time. He was clear that he felt that his parents, especially his mother, were making "a big deal" about his smoking when he thought it was not a problem. He said that he smoked marijuana two or three times a week, sometimes with friends and sometimes alone. He liked feeling high, and he said that it made him feel mellow and helped him get to sleep easier than he would be able to without it.

His parents were concerned that his marijuana use was affecting his performance at school and would therefore limit his college choices. He had about a B average throughout high school, but his grades had begun to dip slightly in the past year. His parents offered to pay for him to take an SAT preparation course, but he refused. Overall, they were frustrated with the direction in which their son was heading. They were perhaps even more concerned, however, with the effect that Bobby's marijuana use was having on his younger siblings, ages fourteen and twelve. The younger kids looked up to Bobby, and the family discord and the firsthand experience of living with a regular marijuana user worried Bobby's parents.

Bobby's impact on his family happens to be the most common clinical picture I see in the marijuana-related consultations I do for my private practice. Having a young family member get into trouble related to marijuana use is often a family's first exposure to addiction, so it is understandable that they often are not familiar with the next steps. Most of the time, parents become concerned about marijuana use sooner than their child does, so there is a clear divide in attitude toward marijuana use during the consultation. As mentioned earlier, young people often need to have several bad outcomes occur before they grasp the severity of the situation. It is usually only when young people risk losing something tangible that they want—admission to a particular college, eligibility for a sports team at their school—that they begin to understand the predicament they are in.

Making an effort to learn about marijuana addiction and the steps necessary to treat it can be arduous and often scary. Parents expend a lot of energy worrying about their children, what having an addiction might mean, and whether they will be able to find effective treatment that can help their son or daughter. It is especially frustrating when that concern and energy level is not matched by the child. I have seen many sets of parents get worn down by the entire treatment process when their child does not appear as invested as the parents in achieving a successful treatment outcome.

The potential impact of marijuana addiction on the young

person's siblings, especially younger siblings, is concerning as well. While parents and the choices they make about drug use are clearly role models for their children, older siblings are role models for younger siblings as well. The similarity in age and closeness of the relationship may even result in the older sibling being more influential than the child's parents. Bobby's parents were justified in their worry about the effects of his use on the family's younger children.

Parents can minimize the negative effects of a situation like this by being clear about both their opinion of marijuana use and their willingness to help a child who needs help. There are many factors that play into the decisions that kids make about whether or not to use marijuana when they are in their teens, but parents providing a clear, firm message that they think marijuana use among young people is a bad idea reduces the likelihood that their child will decide to use. Similarly, showing a desire to help under any circumstances makes it more likely that a child will come to them down the road if they are having problems.

Family and Friends Must Protect Themselves

As we have seen throughout the course of this book, battling addiction is exhausting and helping someone in this battle also takes a tremendous toll. But just as you must put on your own oxygen mask before helping others with theirs, family and friends must take steps to protect themselves while trying to help their loved one battle marijuana addiction. This protection should occur both psychologically and physically.

Similar to the message from chapter 8, "Never Worry Alone," family members should seek psychological support in dealing with their loved ones' addiction. I strongly encourage family members to see a therapist knowledgeable in addictions either individually, as a couple, or as a group. This therapy is often the first time that family members have ever talked with a professional therapist about addiction and their response to it, which greatly increases the likelihood that the therapy will be very useful. There will be many points along the way in which family members will face difficult decisions, and therapists can be incredibly valuable in helping people make those decisions and deal with the psychological aftermath. Guilt, for example, can be overwhelming at times for family members dealing with addiction, and it is very helpful to have an unbiased expert help family members examine their feelings about the difficult decisions they have had to make.

Self-help groups are also important tools to help family members address their loved ones' addiction. Self-help groups can be used as adjunctive treatment to individual therapy; if finances or insurance coverage allows, it can be more productive for family members to start with individual therapy and then add self-help groups to the schedule. Al-Anon, www.al-anon.alateen.org, helps loved ones find understanding and support from others who are facing the same addiction problems that they are. Nar-Anon, www.nar-anon.org/naranon, is a national self-help organization that helps families address drug use. Learn to Cope, www.learn2cope.org, offers similar support on a local scale. Some treatment facilities and hospitals offer programs for family members as well. McLean Hospital, where I work, has a meeting every Monday night and one Saturday a month that is solely for the family members of those who have been in our substance abuse treatment program. This group is very popular and makes it possible for everyone in the family affected by addiction to face their struggles together instead of alone.

Psychotherapy encourages family members to continue to learn about addiction and themselves. Learning about addiction from the right sources prepares family members for the battle ahead. Having an idea about what might occur in a given situation increases the likelihood of positive outcomes. Being more educated about addiction also makes family members greater assets for self-help groups as well.

Having someone you love battle addiction is a constant stressor that can go on for extended periods of time. During those periods, it is important for family members to be vigilant about taking care of themselves physically with appropriate sleep and exercise, along with a proper diet. Being rested and strong puts family members in a better position to expend their energy helping their loved one with addiction. It is easy to think that you do not have time for exercise, for example, in stressful times. But the hour spent taking a walk or doing yoga will enhance the rest of the hours in your week.

Summary

When thinking about marijuana addiction, it is easy to be consumed by the effects that the addiction has on the person with the addiction. But marijuana addiction affects many more people than just the user, including family, spouses, and friends, so it is important to think about how this addiction affects others and the things that loved ones can do to minimize the negative impact that marijuana addiction can have on them. Those affected by marijuana addiction should seek individual psychotherapy in order to think through the decisions they are making and the feelings that come with those decisions. Self-help groups not only help to educate family members dealing with addiction, but they also help to reinforce the notion that there are millions of others who have dealt with and are dealing with addiction in their lives just as you are. In addition to seeking psychological help for their experiences with addiction, family and friends should also make an effort to take care of themselves physically.

CONCLUSION

Where Do We Go from Here?

As I recounted in the preface, my family history and, more recently, my experiences with patients and families have helped make me passionate about marijuana and addiction. Many people either think that "marijuana" and "addiction" go together all of the time or none of the time, and now you know that the truth falls somewhere in the gray area. The gap between the scientific truths about marijuana and the public perception is what motivated me to write this book. In this final chapter, I'd like to reinforce the complexity of the issues surrounding marijuana and ultimately help you understand the direction I feel we, as a society, should be moving in with this extraordinary substance.

What We Need: Evidence-Based Public Policy

While no one knows for sure how the issues related to marijuana will play out, we do know that we are entering a critical period. The decisions made by our politicians and the decisions we make in the voting booths will go a long way toward shaping the future of marijuana policy in the United States. I'd like to think that by reading this book, you have learned more about marijuana than you knew previously and, because of this, you are in a better position to make educated decisions about the future of that policy. There are reasons to be both concerned and hopeful about the future.

As for timing, it is hard to imagine things will not get worse before they get better. The majority of Americans, as the votes have attested around the country, are in favor of increased access to marijuana. They support decriminalization, medical marijuana, and legalization by a wide margin, so much so that it seems likely that more and more states will enact medical marijuana laws, just as increasing numbers of states will put the question of legalization of marijuana on their ballots. This is problematic when considered in the context of the major surveys of young people that are conducted annually. The data noted earlier from the Monitoring the Future survey, conducted by researchers from the University of Michigan, is potentially concerning.[59] It shows that among our young people, use of marijuana is on the rise while use of every other illicit drug is on the decline. As marijuana use among young people is on an upward trend, the perception of risk among this group is also declining. There is a link between young people's perception of risk and their willingness to try a drug.

While there are many potential explanations for this trend, including public sentiments about the harmfulness of marijuana, discussion about medical marijuana and legalization of marijuana, and the marijuana use habits of influential musicians, actors, and athletes, it seems nearly impossible to turn things around immediately. Thus, these factors point toward the trend of increased marijuana use and decreased perception of risk continuing at least for the next few years. This may be difficult for some to accept, given that the data showing the potential harms of marijuana is clear, strong, and growing. As we have discussed elsewhere in this book, however, most people are not aware of how potentially dangerous marijuana can be, and this is why educational efforts, which we will describe later, are so important moving forward. We want people to know the facts so they can make educated choices about whether to use marijuana or how they will vote on the issues of medical marijuana and legalization.

To clarify, the problem is not that people support issues such as medical marijuana and legalization of marijuana; it's that their support of these issues is often buoyed by flawed logic and very little science. After studying the research, looking at policy, and treating many people with addiction to marijuana, I have come to the conclusion that medical marijuana and legalization of marijuana are feasible ideas *depending on how the regulations are written.* As they stand at the time of this writing, with medical marijuana laws enacted in twenty-three states and the District of Columbia, and the recreational use of marijuana becoming legal in an increasing number of states, the policy is ahead of the science. This is an unfortunate predicament.

Let's revisit a few things about medical marijuana and legalized marijuana. With medical marijuana, there are indeed medical conditions for which there is scientific data compelling enough to warrant the use of medical marijuana. Chronic pain, neuropathic pain, and the spasticity associated with multiple sclerosis are examples of such conditions where medical marijuana may make sense if other treatment options have been tried and failed. With legalization, as I mentioned previously, I just don't think you can seriously consider it today when issues such as driving safety and the impact of legalization on addiction have not been ironed out. Washington and Colorado are desperately trying to sort out many complicated issues after implementing the laws.

Try to look at this from the perspective of a doctor who is concerned about the safety and well-being of his or her patients. As a society, our rush to "medicalize" and legalize marijuana puts citizens at risk. As a physician who conducts clinical trials,

I understand the importance of following procedures that are designed to limit risk to participants. My studies require approvals from the Food and Drug Administration, the National Institute on Drug Abuse, and the McLean Hospital Institutional Review Board, and my colleagues and I must take numerous extra steps, both in the way we conduct the studies and with the paperwork we are required to complete, in order to reduce the chances that participants might be harmed. We accept these extra steps because we understand their importance, which is why it is difficult to watch as the current legalization laws put citizens at risk. The steps take time and they slow the pace of our research—*but they protect our patients from harm.*

I wish we had a similar approach to the public policy surrounding marijuana: careful research leading to policy that is developed and implemented gradually in a way that minimizes risks while balancing medical needs and personal liberty. While the ideas behind medical marijuana and legalization of marijuana may have merit, their implementation is troubling. Creating regulations to guide states' implementation of these ideas is not easy, and there are myriad issues to consider. But state after state has implemented medical marijuana regulations with serious flaws. For example, California allows physicians to recommend medical marijuana for whatever medical problem they choose, whether there is data to support the use of medical marijuana for the problem or not. In Massachusetts, a patient may possess up to ten ounces of marijuana every sixty days, which is enough marijuana to roll 560 joints.

There are likely many causes for this haphazard, flawed implementation:

- Many people have strong financial stakes in how (or whether) these marijuana policies are implemented.

- The public health commissions that create the regulations may lack enough input from experts in the field.

- Votes to legalize, decriminalize, or allow medical marijuana are cast on ballot measures that are stated too simply.

- The public seeking change has not been given the facts that allow citizens to consider nuanced legislation, and public forums themselves do not favor nuanced discussion.

- The political process is set up to favor simplified, polarized positions rather than considered, balanced, and complex ones.

No matter what the reason, the regulations have been lacking and it has taken many states years to implement the wishes of the voters. Similarly, as we mentioned above, it is worrisome that, as I write this, four states have already moved forward with legalization and many more are considering doing so, without the data necessary to create a legalization system that would limit risk.

The vitriol surrounding the marijuana debate has hindered the development of effective policies. There is a great deal of passion on both sides of this issue, but there seems to have been little attempt to compromise thus far. Both sides of the debate lobby policymakers hard, and then the policymakers make decisions that at times lack solid rationale. It would be helpful if members from each side could be trusted to attempt to compromise on these issues and then be allowed to play a more active role in constructing the regulations. Alternatively, each side could propose places in the regulations on which they would be willing to compromise. Clearly, the current scenario where many on both sides of the debate cherry-pick data and sling rhetoric back and forth has not borne fruit.

What We Need: Evidence-Based Help
for Users and Their Loved Ones

Unfortunately, there is no agreed-upon effective treatment for marijuana addiction at a time when we face increasing numbers of people with this addiction. There is a long road before us in the battle to help those with marijuana addiction make significant reductions in their use, but we are in need of help now. We reviewed a number of promising medications (see appendix A for a list), some of which are already available in the United States, but we need more research that produces effective medications, and ideally a medication that has FDA approval for marijuana addiction, now. For the roughly one out of every ten adults (and one out of six teens) who do develop addiction after using, marijuana is a *very* serious problem. The social toll on personal lives, family, friends, employers, and co-workers is enormous—as are the associated costs. Having effective medications available would allow us to let those who may want treatment know that we are here to help them and that we have proven treatments at our disposal.

There are reasons to be hopeful about where marijuana policy and the treatment of marijuana addiction are headed, however. Important, groundbreaking research is being done in several areas—epidemiology, effects of marijuana use, treatment of marijuana addiction, and the use of cannabinoids to treat medical problems. For example, clinical trials evaluating cannabinoids as treatments for medical problems will be essential moving forward. Some of this research is being done currently as pharmaceutical companies strive to bring new cannabinoids to market with expanded medical purposes, or indications. It seems likely that we will have some exciting new cannabinoids available in the U.S. market within the next five years. Of course, the availability of these new cannabinoids will likely alter the role of the marijuana plant in the treatment of various medical problems. We need more research, clearly, but fortunately people are starting to recognize this. For example, many have pointed to the federal policy controlling and criminalizing marijuana as a "Schedule I" drug—meaning it has no medical value and high abuse potential—as a hindrance to research on marijuana and cannabinoids. Though marijuana does have a high abuse potential (like many prescription painkillers and like alcohol), at this point we have evidence that marijuana has medical value. For perspective, dronabinol and nabilone, cannabinoids that are being studied for a variety of medical purposes, are not as fiercely regulated as marijuana.*

Exciting epidemiological studies have been done in the past two decades to evaluate the relationship of marijuana with a variety of psychiatric disorders and medical conditions. At least some of these studies show links between marijuana use and a number of problems, especially when use starts at a young age. These types of studies need to be replicated. They also need to be used to inform our policies regarding decriminalization, medical marijuana, and legalization of marijuana. For example, the study by Dr. Madeleine Meier from Duke University and her collaborators that showed up to an eight-point decline in IQ as a result of early, regular marijuana use has been hotly debated.[60] While there are other studies that demonstrate the dangers of early, regular marijuana use among young people, we are in need of additional large long-term studies like Meier's. Recent work by Dr. Jodi Gilman and her colleagues at Massachusetts General Hospital showing structural brain changes in

---

* Nabilone is rated as Schedule II, and dronabinol is rated as Schedule III by the federal government. A Schedule II drug is considered to have a high potential for abuse, but not as high as Schedule I. Well-known Schedule II drugs include cocaine, oxycodone, methamphetamine, fentanyl, Adderall, and Ritalin. Schedule III drugs are considered to have moderate to low potential for physical or psychological dependence and include drugs such as steroids, ketamine, and mixtures that contain low levels of some higher-schedule drugs, such as Tylenol III and Vicodin. Drug scheduling has an impact on use, distribution, research, and other aspects of a drug's "life."

occasional marijuana users has opened the door for more work to answer questions about the effects of occasional marijuana use in young people.[61] This work is especially relevant due to millions of people who use marijuana, but don't have an addiction to it.

Additional research on the effects of marijuana on driving is also sorely needed. Not only do we need larger studies of the immediate impact of using marijuana on driving, but we need to figure out the effects of marijuana use on driving within different windows of time. We must determine reliably how a certain dose of marijuana affects driving depending on when the dose was taken. We have some of this information, but it is crucial to try to solidify the existing data as more Americans use medical marijuana and legalized recreational marijuana.

We also need additional clinical trials aimed toward developing behavioral interventions and medications for those addicted to marijuana. A goal of my research is to develop either an effective behavioral intervention or medication that will enable those who are addicted to have a good chance of stopping if they want to stop. As more people become aware that marijuana is addictive and that people can develop problems in multiple areas of their lives due to their marijuana use, more people will come forward seeking help. It is hard to muster the courage to seek help for something when you hear from your friends and the media that it isn't really a problem.

What We Need: Evidence-Based Prevention Programs

An additional emphasis must be placed on improved, evidence-based education about marijuana. This should be a multipronged approach that includes delivering a consistent message at schools, places of worship, doctors' offices, and in other community settings like health fairs. For example, I have partnered with the Boston Public Schools and their Health and Wellness Department to bring evidence-based education about the potential dangers of marijuana to all ninth- and tenth-graders in their thirty-three high schools. School administrators have clamored for this type of program, but evidence-based marijuana education needs to be integrated into health curriculums, and educational efforts can't be a once-a-year undertaking. Instead there needs to be educational content specifically tailored to a particular school with regular follow-up. Bringing in celebrities to talk about their history might fill a gymnasium, but a sustained program with repeated contacts between health experts and teachers throughout the year is what leads to measurable change. We will need broader support from local and national leaders to accomplish this program of expanded, evidence-based education, and we may even need to incentivize people to attend—sometimes we all need an extra push to do things we know we should do. Our educational efforts will need to come more from formal channels, thereby increasing the percentage of information provided by experts on evidence-based best practices and decreasing the percentage from social media or television.

Education about marijuana should emphasize the science and not the half-truths presented in the past or the rhetoric put forth by the pro- and anti-marijuana groups. We must carefully examine what we've done right and what we've done wrong with alcohol and tobacco and determine how to apply this to marijuana. While there are positive and negative aspects to our policies on alcohol and tobacco, the trends for use of those two drugs are decreasing, so it appears that we are doing more of the right things than the wrong things. For example, we should try to stop glamorizing the use of marijuana and instead portray it as the potentially harmful and addictive drug that it is, in the same way that we have shifted the public perception of cigarette smoking. It seems likely that more states will enact medical marijuana and recreational marijuana laws. If that is the case, then we should gradually make it more difficult and expensive to use marijuana, just as excise taxes have made it more expensive to smoke cigarettes. The costs associated with marijuana use—taxes and costs for addiction treatment, for example—should be shared by all involved in the production, sale, and use of marijuana.

Our public attitude toward marijuana needs to change. This starts with as many people as possible knowing the truth about marijuana. The public attitude should be clear: marijuana is potentially harmful and addictive. Just as we do not need advertising for alcohol for people to understand its appeal, we don't need advertising or glamorization of marijuana. Adults who want to use know about it and will use it, hopefully in a responsible manner. They don't need any encouragement to do so.

To close, I'd like to share one more story about a former patient of mine.

Ricky

Ricky is a twenty-one-year-old young man with a history of depression. He was brought to me by his parents when he was seventeen because he had been expelled from his second high school in large part due to his marijuana use. His parents were desperate and willing to do anything to help him; he had already been in multiple treatment programs prior to seeing me. While we found something in common being basketball fans, I suspect that Ricky was not thrilled about seeing me weekly for a couple of months before he was to start at his third high school. While I adjusted his antidepressant dose, we mostly talked in great detail about his marijuana use and his difficulties at school. I listened to Ricky and it became clear to me that he was tired of messing up and he wanted to try hard to succeed for both his parents and himself. He and his parents were scared— scared about what would happen if he did not stop using. While they were actively seeking the best treatment they could find, they also felt helpless to some degree. That resonated with me and it still does; I think about my grandfather and my uncle and then my own daughters and how, although you can try as hard as you can to fight addiction, success is far from guaranteed. I fight against that feeling of helplessness that is present when addiction takes a life; it is a somber and empty feeling.

Ricky made it out of the difficult position he had been in when I met him, and he is now a student at a college in the region. His parents have done me the favor of keeping me apprised of his progress. They say that he drinks alcohol on occasion, and they wonder if he smokes marijuana once in a while as well. Would his parents and I prefer that he not use alcohol or marijuana at all? Sure. But he is doing well in school, his mood is good, and he still sees a therapist every week. And I smile every time I think about him.

Ricky's story is real. It puts a personal face on the issues of our time. Although there are things to be worried about and things to be hopeful about when it comes to the issue of marijuana, this is unquestionably an exciting time of intense interest in marijuana. We can capitalize on this interest by leveraging it to develop educational programs and to fund desperately needed research—on medical uses, on appropriate public policy, and on the best ways to prevent overuse and addiction as marijuana becomes easier to access. We have a tremendous opportunity before us—a chance to find answers to key questions and to teach people what we have learned. The goal is to help develop a public that is knowledgeable about marijuana so they can make more informed choices at home and in the voting booth. Through these steps, perhaps we can cut through the thicket of arguments, polarized positions, and crazy-quilt policies to an approach that is rational, safe, and in the best interests of personal and public well being.

APPENDIX A

Promising Medications for Treating Marijuana Addiction

Dronabinol

Dronabinol (brand name Marinol) is an agonist medication. Dronabinol is a pill composed only of delta-9-tetrahydrocannabinol (THC), the cannabinoid in marijuana that produces the effects that most people are familiar with, including euphoria. It is FDA approved for nausea and vomiting associated with cancer chemotherapy as well as appetite stimulation in wasting illnesses such as AIDS. As with other agonist medications, the idea behind using dronabinol as a medication for marijuana addiction is to prevent withdrawal symptoms by occupying the same nerve cell receptors (cannabinoid 1 receptors in this case) occupied when one smokes marijuana. (We discussed how nerve cell receptors work in chapter 7. See figure 4, "Cannabinoids plug in to receptor sites in brain cells," on page 101.) When a marijuana smoker abruptly stops their regular use of marijuana, the unoccupied receptors play a role in triggering withdrawal symptoms. As we discussed in chapter 5, unpleasant withdrawal symptoms like anxiety, irritability, and insomnia may lead someone who is trying to stop use of marijuana to relapse in order to make the withdrawal symptoms go away.

Dronabinol as a treatment for marijuana addiction has been studied in one large clinical trial conducted by Dr. Frances Levin and her colleagues at Columbia University. In Dr. Levin's study, participants with marijuana addiction took forty milligrams of dronabinol daily over a twelve-week period.[62] Although treatment with dronabinol did not result in greater abstinence from marijuana during the clinical trial, those who took dronabinol as opposed to a placebo were more likely to complete the study and they had fewer marijuana withdrawal symptoms during it. While this research did not produce an overwhelmingly positive result, dronabinol should be studied further as a treatment for marijuana addiction. One clinical trial, particularly one with some positive results, should not be the basis for eliminating a medication as a possible effective treatment, especially considering the strong conceptual rationale for using it.

Coincidentally, in a small preliminary clinical trial, my research team is studying dronabinol in combination with another medication, clonidine, as a possible treatment for patients with both marijuana addiction and psychotic disorders such as schizophrenia or schizoaffective disorder.

One of the problems with using dronabinol to aid in the treatment of marijuana addiction is that dronabinol is just THC, the primary active ingredient in marijuana. This means that a person who is being treated with dronabinol who takes urine test for marijuana will have a positive result—even if he or she hasn't used marijuana. Urine tests can be part of treatment protocols, work requirements, or other situations where a person needs to demonstrate that he or she isn't using marijuana. The fact that dronabinol will show up as marijuana use on a drug screening limits its applications in treatment.

Nabiximols

There are other promising cannabinoids being studied as agonist treatments for marijuana addiction as well. Nabiximols (brand name Sativex) is an oral spray that contains the two major active cannabinoids in the marijuana plant, THC and cannabidiol (CBD), in nearly a 1:1 ratio.[63] The presence of both THC and CBD makes nabiximols an especially exciting medication because it more closely resembles the marijuana plant than any other cannabinoid medication available. Nabiximols is currently being studied as a treatment for marijuana addiction in a clinical trial in Australia. There is a good chance that nabiximols will receive FDA approval in the United States within the next few years, although it will be approved for medical purposes other than marijuana addiction, at least initially.

Nabilone

Nabilone (brand name Cesamet) is another cannabinoid agonist that has promise as a medication for marijuana addiction. Nabilone, like dronabinol, is a medication that can be taken by people trying to stop using marijuana to lessen withdrawal symptoms during their quit attempt. As a treatment medication, nabilone would be taken for a period of a couple months and then gradually tapered off under the supervision of a doctor. A key potential advantage to nabilone over dronabinol is that nabilone does not produce a positive marijuana urine drug screen. Because nabilone does not contain THC, if someone were prescribed nabilone to stop using marijuana and then managed to completely stop using, his or her urine drug screen could be completely negative. So the urine drug screen would be a more useful tool in nabilone treatment than in dronabinol treatment. Our research group at McLean Hospital recently completed a preliminary clinical trial funded by the National Institute on Drug Abuse using nabilone as a medication for marijuana addiction, and a larger second study is about to commence.

N-acetylcysteine

When there are no FDA-approved medications for a particular medical condition, oftentimes researchers will study medications with a variety of mechanisms in an effort to find some thing that works. In the field of addiction, that has famously been the case in the hunt for a medication to treat cocaine addiction. No stone has been left unturned in that hunt. This same approach, though to a lesser degree thus far, has been used in trying to find a medication for marijuana addiction. This outside-the-box philosophy has led to the uncovering of some promising medications.

N-acetylcysteine is one of these promising medications. N-acetylcysteine has a variety of medical uses, although it is most known for its use as an antidote for acetaminophen (brand name Tylenol) overdoses. N-acetylcysteine is mostly purchased over the counter as a health supplement. N-acetylcysteine is a "precursor" to the amino acid cysteine, which means that it can be converted to cysteine in the body. Cysteine is thought to be involved in the transmission in the brain of the neurotransmitter, or brain chemical, glutamate. Glutamate is a powerful neurotransmitter that is likely to play a role in addiction and, as such, medications that affect glutamate have been studied for a variety of addictive disorders. In one study, Dr. Kevin Gray and colleagues at the Medical University of South Carolina had 116 adolescents with marijuana addiction take 1,200 milligrams a day of N-acetylcysteine or a corresponding placebo (sugar pill) during an eight-week clinical trial.[64] The participants in the study did not know whether they were receiving the real drug or the sugar pill. Gray and his colleagues found that the participants taking N-acetylcysteine were significantly more likely to produce a marijuana-free urine drug screen at the end of the eight-week trial than those taking a placebo sugar pill. This is evidence that N-acetylcysteine may help people reduce their marijuana use. Due to these promising results, the National Institute on Drug Abuse is currently conducting a larger clinical trial in multiple medical centers across the country in an effort to get a definitive answer as to whether more physicians should be recommending N-acetylcysteine as a medication for those who want to stop using marijuana.

Gabapentin

Gabapentin (brand name Neurontin) is another medication that has produced promising results in a clinical trial for marijuana addiction. Gabapentin is structurally related to the brain chemical gamma-amino-butyric acid (GABA). Gabapentin is thought to directly affect the transport of GABA by blocking a cellular calcium channel involved in this pathway. Gabapentin, like N-acetylcysteine above, has been used to treat a wide variety of medical conditions, although it is FDA approved as a treatment for seizure disorders. Dr. Barbara Mason and colleagues at the Scripps Research Institute in La Jolla, California, conducted a clinical trial in which adults with marijuana addiction were given either 1,200 milligrams of gabapentin daily or a placebo over a twelve-week period.[65] This study of moderate size produced positive results. Participants who took gabapentin had statistically significant reductions in marijuana use (both in grams used and in days of use) when compared to the placebo group. The gabapentin group also experienced reductions in marijuana withdrawal symptoms, marijuana cravings, sleep difficulties, and scores on depression scales. They also improved cognitively on measures of executive functioning. Overall, while larger clinical trials of gabapentin as a treatment for marijuana addiction are needed, this study suggests that gabapentin, which has a favorable side effect profile, might be a useful low-risk, high-potential reward medication that can be used as a part of a comprehensive treatment plan.

Buspirone

Buspirone (brand name Buspar) is an anti-anxiety medication that has also been studied in a moderate-sized clinical trial for the treatment of marijuana addiction.[66] Fifty participants received sixty milligrams daily of buspirone or a placebo over a twelve-week treatment trial. The results showed a slightly higher percentage of marijuana-free urine drug screens among those receiving buspirone. Due to the small size of the study, we don't know if the results are strong enough to indicate that the drug may be useful in marijuana treatment. A larger study will be needed to suggest whether these early results hold promise. A benefit is that buspirone, like gabapentin, is well tolerated by patients and produces few side effects, making it a medication worth considering when trying to help someone stop marijuana use.

More drugs under study

A number of other medications have been studied in clinical trials as treatments for marijuana addiction without positive results. Nefazodone and sustained-release bupropion, two medications that are FDA approved for the treatment of depression, were studied in a clinical trial of 116 adults with marijuana addiction but these medications did not produce results that were different from the placebo in the areas of marijuana use and marijuana withdrawal symptoms.[67] Venlafaxine is another FDA-approved medication for the treatment of depression and multiple forms of anxiety disorders that was studied in adults with both marijuana addiction and low mood. In this study, the participants assigned to the venlafaxine group actually did worse than the participants in the placebo group.[68] Divalproex, a medication that is FDA approved for the treatment of seizure disorders, has also been studied in a trial that included more than twenty-five participants.[69] This six-week clinical trial showed no difference between divalproex and the placebo in terms of marijuana use. There have been other preliminary studies of the drugs baclofen, sustained-release bupropion, divalproex, mirtazapine, and nefazodone. However, the studies had twenty or fewer participants and the results were not conclusive.

While the medications described above are not FDA approved as treatments for marijuana addiction and can only be used off-label for this purpose, many groups are working hard to make effective medications available. Research on other mental illnesses like depression suggests that patients fare better on a combination of behavioral therapy and medication than they would with treatment of either one alone. Ultimately, we expect that, as with these other illnesses, a combination of a behavioral intervention or talk therapy with a medication will be the treatment of choice for marijuana addiction.

APPENDIX B

Signs That a Child May Be Using

Here are some indicators that your child may be using marijuana. He or she may

- seem dizzy or uncoordinated
- seem silly and giggly for no reason
- have very red, bloodshot eyes
- have a hard time remembering things that just happened
- be in possession of drugs and drug paraphernalia, including pipes and rolling papers
- have an odor of marijuana smoke on clothes and in the bedroom
- use incense and other deodorizers to mask the smell of marijuana smoke
- use eye drops
- wear clothing or jewelry or have posters that promote drug use
- have expenditures

More general signs of use include the following:

- declining school work and grades
- loss of motivation

- loss of pleasure from former activities
- abrupt changes in choice of friends, groups, or behavior
- change in sleeping habits
- abnormal health issues
- deteriorating relationships with family
- less openness and honesty

Of course, a growing teen may be uncoordinated, silly, forgetful, and so forth *without* drugs. Use your judgment, don't leap to conclusions, and watch for an accumulation of signs. If you suspect use, talk to your child, set clear boundaries and expectations, and be ready to seek help if the behaviors do not change. Your job is to support and protect your child. If you spot serious signs of drug effects (such as nausea, vomiting, hallucinations, psychoses), call 911 immediately. For nonthreatening situations, when you discover alcohol, marijuana, or other evidence of drug use, here are some actions you could take:

- Let your child know you are concerned and that you disapprove.
- Set limits and consequences.
- Monitor their behavior and physical signs of use.
- Get outside help. The Substance Abuse and Mental Health Services Administration has a free helpline at 1-800-662-HELP (4357). The website is www.samhsa.gov.

Source:
Get Smart about Marijuana: A Hazelden Quick Guide (Hazelden Publishing, 2013)

RECOMMENDED READING

Caulkins, J. P., A. Hawken, B. Kilmer, and M. Kleiman. *Marijuana Legalization: What Everyone Needs to Know.* New York: Oxford University Press, 2012.

Get Smart About Marijuana. Center City, MN: Hazelden, 2013.

Iversen, Leslie L. *The Science of Marijuana.* New York: Oxford University Press, 2008.

Kleber, H. D., and R. L. Dupont. "Physicians and Medical Marijuana." *American Journal of Psychiatry* 169 (2012): 564–68.

Volkow, N. D., R. D. Baler, W. M. Compton, and S. R. B. Weiss. "Adverse Health Effects of Marijuana." *New England Journal of Medicine* 370 (2014): 2219–27.

NOTES

Chapter 1

1. *Get Smart About Marijuana* (Center City, MN: Hazelden, 2013).

2. Substance Abuse and Mental Health Services Administration, "Results from the 2013 National Survey on Drug Abuse and Health: Summary of National Findings," NSDUH Series H-48, HHS publication no. (SMA) 14-4863 (Rockville, MD: Substance Abuse and Mental Health Services Administration, 2014).

3. Cesamet product information, Meda Pharmaceuticals (Somerset, NJ, 2011); Marinol product information, AbbVie, Inc. (North Chicago, IL, 2013).

4. Center for Behavioral Health Statistics and Quality, *National Survey on Drug Use and Health* (Rockville, MD: Substance Abuse and Mental Health Services Administration, 2013).

5. Kyle Newport, "Ricky Williams Compares Marijuana Use to 'Spinach for Popeye,'" bleacher report, last modified October 8, 2013, http://stag-br-app-s5.brenv.net/articles/1803682-ricky-williams -compares-marijuana-use-to-spinach-for-popeye.

6. Sheila Cosgrove Baylis, "Lady Gaga Admits Having an Addiction to Marijuana," *People*, November 11, 2013, www.people.com /people/article/0,,20754576,00.html.

7. L. D. Johnston, P. M. O'Malley, R. A. Miech, J. G. Bachman, and J. E. Schulenberg, *Monitoring the Future National Results on Drug Use: 1975–2013: Overview, Key Findings on Adolescent Drug Use* (Ann Arbor: Institute for Social Research, University of Michigan, 2014).

8. B. Bracken, J. Rodolico, and K. Hill, "Sex, Age, and Progression of Drug Use in Adolescents Admitted for Substance Use Disorder Treatment in the Northeastern United States: Comparison with a National Survey," *Substance Abuse* 34, no. 3 (2013): 263–72.

9. K. Johnson and R. Chebium, "Justice Dept. Won't Challenge State Marijuana Laws," *USA Today*, August 29, 2013, www.usatoday

.com/story/news/nation/2013/08/29/justice-medical-marijuana-laws /2727605/.

Chapter 2

10. Substance Abuse and Mental Health Services Administration, "Results from the 2011 National Survey on Drug Use and Health: Summary of National Findings." NSDUH series H-44, HHS publication no. (SMA) 12-4713 (Rockville, MD: Substance Abuse and Mental Health Services Administration, 2012).

11. Substance Abuse and Mental Health Services Administration, "Results from the 2011 National Survey on Drug Use and Health."

12. Louisa Degenhardt, Harvey A. Whiteford, Alize J. Ferrari, Amanda J. Baxter, Fiona J. Charlson, Wayne D. Hall, Greg Freedman et al., "Global burden of disease attributable to illicit drug use and dependence: findings from the Global Burden of Disease Study 2010," *Lancet* 382, no. 9904 (2013): 1564-74.

13. James C. Anthony, Lynn A. Warner, and Ronald C. Kessler, "Comparative Epidemiology of Dependence on Tobacco, Alcohol, Controlled Substances, and Inhalants: Basic Findings from the National Comorbidity Survey," *Experimental and Clinical Psychopharmacology* 2, no. 3 (1994): 244–68; Catalina Lopez-Quintero, José Pérez de los Cobos, Deborah S. Hasin, Mayumi Okuda, Shuai Wang, Bridget F. Grand, and Carlos Blanco, "Probability and predictors of transition from first use to dependence on nicotine, alcohol, cannabis, and cocaine: Results of the National Epidemiologic Survey on Alcohol and Related Conditions (NESARC)," *Drug and Alcohol Dependence* 115, nos. 1–2, (May 1, 2011): 120–30.

14. Substance Abuse and Mental Health Services Administration, "Results from the 2012 National Survey on Drug Use and Health: Summary of National Findings," NSDUH Series H-46, HHS Publication No. (SMA) 13-4795 (Rockville, MD: Substance Abuse and Mental Health Services Administration, 2013).

Chapter 3

15. Anthony, "Comparative Epidemiology of Dependence on Tobacco, Alcohol, Controlled Substances, and Inhalants," 244–68.

16. Nora D. Volkow, Ruben D. Baler, Wilson M. Compton, and

Susan R. B. Weiss, "Adverse Health Effects of Marijuana Use," *New England Journal of Medicine* 370 (2014): 2219–27.

17. Staci A. Gruber, Kelly A. Sagar, Mary Kathryn Dahlgren, Megan Racine, and Scott E. Lukas, "Age of onset of marijuana use and executive function," *Psychology of Addictive Behaviors* 26 (2012): 496–503.

18. Staci A. Gruber, Mary Kathryn Dahlgren, Kelly A Sagar, Atilla Gönenc, and William D.S. Killgore, "Age of Onset of Marijuana Use Impacts Inhibitory Processing," *Neuroscience Letters* 511, no. 2 (2012): 89–94.

19. Jodi M. Gilman, John K. Kuster, Sang Lee, Myung Joo Lee, Byoung Woo Kim, Nikos Makris, Andre van der Kouwe, Anne J. Blood, and Hans C. Breiter, "Cannabis Use is Quantitatively Associated with Nucleus Accumbens and Amygdala Abnormalities in Young Adult Recreational Users," *The Journal of Neuroscience* 34, no. 16 (2014): 5529–38.

20. Madeline H. Meier, Avshalom Caspi, Antony Ambler, HonaLee Harrington, Renata Houts, Richard S. E. Keefe et al., "Persistent cannabis users show neuropsychological decline from childhood to midlife," *Proceedings of the National Academy of Sciences* 109, no. 40 (2012): E2657–E2664.

21. Robin M. Murray, Paul D. Morrison, Cécile Henquet, and Marta Di Forti, "Cannabis, the mind, and society: the hash realities," *Nature Reviews Neuroscience* 8, no. 11 (2007): 885–95; Ronald C. Kessler, Patricia Burglund, Olga Demler, Robert Jin, Kathleen R. Merikangas, and Ellen E. Walters, "Lifetime prevalence and age-of-onset distributions of DSM-IV disorders in the National Comorbidity Survey Replication," *Archives of General Psychiatry* 62, no. 6 (2005): 593–602.

22. José Alexandre Crippa, Antonio Waldo Zuardi, Rocio Martín-Santos, Sagnik Bhattacharyya, Zerrin Atakan, Philip McGuire, and Paolo Fusar-Poli, "Cannabis and anxiety: A critical review of the evidence," *Human Psychopharmacology: Clinical and Experimental* 24, no. 7 (2009): 515–23.

23. Louisa Degenhardt, Wayne Hall, and Michael Lynskey, "Exploring the association between cannabis use and depression," *Addiction* 98, no. 11 (2003): 1493–1504.

24. Rebecca Kuepper, Jim van Os, Roseline Lieb, Hans-Ulrich Wittchen, Michael Höfler, and Cécile Henquet, "Continued cannabis use and risk of incidence and persistence of psychotic symptoms: 10 year follow-up cohort study," *British Medical Journal* 342 (2011).

25. Matthew Large, Swapnil Sharma, Michael T. Compton, Tim Slade, and Olav Nielssen, "Cannabis Use and Earlier Onset of Psychosis: A Syatematic Meta-analysis," *Archives of General Psychiatry* 68, no. 6 (2011): 555–61.

Chapter 4

26. A. Thomas McLellan, David C. Lewis, Charles P. O'Brien, and Herbert D. Kleber, "Drug Dependence, a Chronic Medical Illness: Implications for Treatment, Insurance, and Outcomes Evaluation," *JAMA* 284, no. 13 (2000): 1689–95.

27. Tom Fowler, Kate Lifford, Katherine Shelton, Frances Rice, Anita Thapar, Michael C. Neale, Andrew McBride, and Marianne B. M. Van Den Bree, "Exploring the relationship between genetic and environmental influences on initiation and progression of substance use," *Addiction* 102, no. 3 (2007): 413–22.

28. Elizabeth J. Santa Ana, Bruce J. Rounsavile, Tami L. Frankorter, Charla Nich, Theresa Babuscio, James Poling, Kishorchandra Gonsai, Kevin P. Hill, Kathleen M. Carroll, "D-Cycloserine attenuates reactivity to smoking cues in nicotine dependent smokers: A pilot investigation," *Drug and Alcohol Dependence* 104, no. 3 (2009): 220–27.

29. Shelly F. Greenfield, Audrey J. Brooks, Susan M. Gordon, Carla A. Green, Frankie Kropp, Kathryn McHugh, Melissa Lincoln, Denise Hien, and Gloria M. Miele, "Substance Abuse Treatment Entry, Retention, and Outcome In Women: A Review of The Literature," *Drug and Alcohol Dependence* 86, no. 1 (2007): 1–21.

Chapter 5

30. R. G. Vandrey, A. J. Budney, J. R. Hughes, and A. Liguori, "A Within-Subject Comparison of Withdrawal Symptoms During Abstinence From Cannabis, Tobacco, and Both Substances," *Drug and Alcohol Dependence* 92, no. 1 (2008): 48–54; Ryan Vandrey, Allen J. Budney, Jody L. Kamon, and Catherine Stanger, "Cannabis with-

drawal in adolescent treatment seekers," *Drug and Alcohol Dependence* 78, no. 2 (2005): 205–10; Alan J. Budney, Ryan G. Vandreym John R. Hughes, Jeff D. Thostenson, and Zoran Bursac, "Comparison of cannabis and tobacco withdrawal: severity and contribution to relapse," *Journal of Substance Abuse Treatment* 35, no. 4 (2008): 362–68.

31. Jeffrey A. Miron, "The Budgetary Implications of Marijuana Prohibition," in *Pot Politics: Marijuana and the Costs of Prohibition* by Mitch Earleywine (Oxford University Press, 2010).

32. Ezekiel Edwards, Will Bunting, and Lynda Garcia, "The War on Marijuana in Black and White" (New York: American Civil Liberties Union, 2013).

33. Marcus A. Bachhuber, Brendan Saloner, Chinazo O. Cunningham, and Colleen L. Barry, "Medical Cannabis Laws and Opioid Analgesic Overdose Mortality in the United States, 1999–2010," *JAMA Internal Medicine* 174, no. 10 (2014): 1668–73.

34. "Tobacco-Related Mortality," Centers for Disease Control and Prevention, last modified February 6, 2014, www.cdc.gov/tobacco /data_statistics/fact_sheets/health_effects/tobacco_related_mortality/.

35. Jennifer M. Whitehill, Frederick P. Rivara, and Megan A. Moreno, "Marijuana-using drivers, alcohol-using drivers, and their passengers: prevalence and risk factors among underage college students," *JAMA Pediatrics* 168, no. 7 (2014): 618–24.

36. R. Andrew Sewell, James Poling, and Mehmet Sofuoglu, "The effect of cannabis compared with alcohol on driving," *American Journal of Addiction* 18, no. 3 (2009): 185–93.

37. World Health Organization, "Cannabis: a health perspective and research agenda" (Geneva: World Health Organization, 1997).

Chapter 7

38. A. B. Ilan, A. Gevens, M. Coleman, M. A. ElSohly, and H. de Wit, "Neurophysiological and subjective profile of marijuana with varying concentrations of cannabinoids," *Behavioural Pharmacology* 16, nos. 5–6 (2005): 487–96.

39. Sagnik Bhatacharyya, Paul D. Morrison, Paolo Fusar-Poli, Rocio Martin-Santos, Stefan Borgwardt, Toby Winton-Brown, and Chiara Nosarti, "Opposite Effects of delta-9-Tetrahydrocannabinol

and Cannabidiol on Human Brain Function and Psychopathology,"
Neuropsychopharmacology 35, no. 3 (2010): 764–74; F. M. Leweke,
D. Piomelli, F. Pahlisch, D. Muhl, C. W. Gerth, C. Hoyer, J. Kloster-
kötter, M. Hellmich, and D Koethe, "Cannabidiol enhances
anadamide signaling and alleviates psychotic symptoms of schizophrenia," *Translational Psychiatry* 2, e94 (2012).

40. Volkow, "Adverse Health Effects of Marijuana Use," 2219–27.

41. Barbara S. Koppel, John C. M. Brust, Terry Fife, Jeff Bronstein,
Sarah Youssof, Gary Gronseth, and David Gloss, "Systematic review:
Efficacy and safety of medical marijuana in selected neurologic
disorders: Report of the Guideline Development Subcommittee of
the American Academy of Neurology," *Neurology* 82, no. 17 (2014):
1556–63.

42. "Should You Be Smoking Marijuana To Treat Your Glaucoma?"
Glaucoma Research Foundation, last modified June 25, 2013,
www.glaucoma.org/treatment/should-you-be-smoking-marijuana
-to-treat-your-glaucoma-1.php.

43. M. Weber, B. Goldman, and S. Truniger, "Tetrahydrocannabi-
nol (THC) for cramps in amyotrophic lateral sclerosis: a randomized,
double-blind crossover trial," *Journal of Neurological Neurosurgery
Psychiatry* 81 (2010): 1135–40.

44. Herbert D. Kleber, and Robert L. DuPont, "Physicians and
Medical Marijuana," *American Journal of Psychiatry* 169, no. 6 (2012):
564–68.

45. Andrew J. Hill, Claire M. Williams, Benjamin J. Whalley, and
Gary J. Stephens, "Phytocannabinoids as novel therapeutic agents
in CNS disorders," *Pharmacology & Therapeutics* 133, no. 1 (2012):
79–97.

46. Massachusetts Department of Public Health "105 CMR 725.000:
Implementation of an act for the humanitarian medical use of marijuana," last modified May 8, 2013, www.mass.gov/eohhs/docs/dph
/regs/105cmr725.pdf.

47. Charles R. Phillips and Lon N. Larson, "Evaluating the Oper-
ational Performance and Financial Effects of a Drug Prior Authorization Program," *Journal of Managed Care Pharmacy* 3, no. 6 (1997):
699–719.

48. Stacy Salomonsen-Sautel, Joseph T. Sakai, Christian Thur-

stone, Robin Corley, and Christian Hopfer, "Medical Marijuana Use Among Adolescents in Substance Abuse Treatment," *Journal of the American Academy of Child and Adolescent Psychiatry* 51, no. 7 (2012): 694–702.

49. Kevin P. Hill, "Medical Marijuana: More Questions than Answers," *Journal of Psychiatric Practice* 20, no. 5 (2014): 389–91.

50. James Sunshine, "Denver Now Has More Marijuana Dispensaries Than It Does Starbucks," *Huffington Post,* July 6, 2012, www.huffingtonpost.com/2011/07/06/medical-marijuana-denver -starbucks_n_891796.html.

Chapter 8

51. Kessler, Burglund, Demler, Jin, Merikangas, and Walters, "Lifetime prevalence and age-of-onset distributions of DSM-IV disorders in the National Comorbidity Survey Replication," 593–602.

52. American Psychiatric Association, *Diagnostic and Statistical Manual of Mental Disorders, 5th ed.* (Washington, DC: 2013).

53. Stephen Rollnick and William R. Miller, "What is motivational interviewing?," *Behavioural and Cognitive Psychotherapy* 23 (1995): 325–34.

54. Kevin P. Hill, "After Detoxification: Levels of Treatment for Alcohol Dependence," *American Family Physician* 88, no. 9 (2013): 589–95.

Chapter 9

55. Project MATCH Research Group, "Matching Alcoholism Treatments to Client Heterogeneity: Project MATCH Three-Year Drinking Outcomes," *Alcoholism: Clinical and Experimental Research* 22 (1998): 1300–1311.

56. Kathleen M. Carroll, Caroline J. Easton, Charla Nich, Karen A. Hunkele, Tara M. Neavins, Rajita Sinha, Haley L. Ford, Sally A. Vitolo, Cheryl A. Doebrick, and Bruce J. Rounsaville, "The Use of Contingency Management and Motivational/Skills-Building Therapy to Treat Young Adults with Marijuana Dependence," *Journal of Consulting and Clinical Psychology* 74, no. 5 (2006): 955–66.

57. Howard A. Liddle, Gayle A. Dakof, Ralph M. Turner, Craig E. Henderson, and Paul E. Greenbaum, "Treating adolescent drug abuse:

a randomized trial comparing multidimensional family therapy and cognitive behavior therapy," *Addiction* 103, no. 10 (2008): 1660–70.

58. Kevin P. Hill, Heather E. Bennett, Margaret L. Griffin, Hilary S. Connery, Garrett M. Fitzmaurice, Geetha Subramaniam, George E. Woody, and Roger D. Weiss, "Association of Cannabis Use with Opioid Outcomes among Opioid-Dependent Youth," *Drug and Alcohol Dependence* 132, nos. 1–2 (2013): 342–5.

Conclusion

59. Johnston, O'Malley, Miech, Bachman, and Schulenberg, *Monitoring the Future.*

60. Meier, Caspi, Ambler, Harrington, Houts, Keefe et al., "Persistent cannabis users show neuropsychological decline."

61. Jodi M. Gilman, John K. Kuster, Sang Lee, Myung Joo Lee, Byoung Woo Kim, Nikos Makris, Andre ver der Kouwe, Anne J. Blood, and Hans C. Breiter, "Cannabis Use Is Quantitatively Associated with Nucleus Accumbens and Amygdala Abnormalities in Young Adult Recreational Users," *The Journal of Neuroscience* 34, no. 16 (2014): 5529–38.

Appendix A

62. Frances R. Levin, John J. Mariani, Daniel J. Brooks, Matina Pavlicova, Wendy Cheng, and Edward Nunes, "Dronabinol for the Treatment of Cannabis Dependence: A Randomized, Double-Blind, Placebo-Controlled Trial," *Drug and Alcohol Dependence* 116, nos. 1–3 (2011): 142–50.

63. "Sativex Oromucosal Spray," Electronic medicines compendium, last modified March 7, 2014, www.medicines.org.uk/emc /medicine/23262.

64. Kevin M. Gray, Matthew J. Carpenter, Nathaniel L. Baker, Stacia M. DeSantis, Elisabeth Kryway, Karen J. Hartwill, Aimee L. McRae-Clark, and Kathleen T. Brady, "A double-blind randomized controlled trial of N-acetylcysteine in cannabis-dependent adolescents," *American Journal of Psychiatry* 169, no. 8 (2012): 805–12.

65. Barbara J. Mason, Rebecca Crean, Vivian Goodell, John M. Light, Susan Quello, Farhad Shadan, Kimberly Buffkins et al., "A Proof-of-Concept Randomized Controlled Study of Gabapentin:

Effects on Cannabis Use, Withdrawal and Executive Function Deficits in Cannabis-Dependent Adults," *Neuropsychopharmacology* 37, no. 7 (2012): 1689–98.

66. Aimee L. McRae-Clark, Rickey E. Carter, Therese K. Killeen, Matthew J. Carpenter, Amy E. Wahlquist, Stacey A. Simpson, and Kathleen T. Brady, "A Placebo-Controlled Trial of Buspirone for the Treatment of Marijuana Dependence," *Drug and Alcohol Dependence* 105, nos. 1–2 (2009): 132–8.

67. Kenneth M. Carpenter, David McDowell, Daniel J. Brooks, Wendy Cheng, and Frances R. Levin, "A Preliminary Trial: Double-Blind Comparison of Nefazodone, Bupropion-SR, and Placebo in the Treatment of Cannabis Dependence," *American Journal of Addiction* 18, no. 1 (2009): 53–64.

68. Frances R. Levin, John Mariani, Daniel J. Brooks, Martna Pavlicova, Edward V. Nunes, Vito Agosti, Adam Bisaga, Maria A. Sullivan, and Kenneth M. Carpenter, "A Randomized Double-Blind, Placebo-Controlled Trial of Venlafaxine-Extended Release for Co-occurring Cannabis Dependence and Depressive Disorders," *Addiction* 108, no. 6 (2013): 1084–94.

69. Frances Rudnick Levin, David McDowell, Suzette M. Evans, Edward Nunes, Evaristo Akerele, Stephen Donovan, and Suzanne K. Vosburg, "Pharmacotherapy for marijuana dependence: a double-blind, placebo-controlled pilot study of divalproex sodium," *American Journal of Addiction* 13, no. 1 (2004): 21–32.

ABOUT THE AUTHOR

Kevin P. Hill, MD, MHS, is an assistant professor of psychiatry at Harvard's McLean Hospital in Belmont, Massachusetts, and an addiction consultant with a number of professional sports organizations. His marijuana research is funded by the NIH, the Brain and Behavior Research Foundation, and the American Lung Association. In 2013 he was awarded the Alfred Pope Award for Best Research Paper by a Young Investigator at McLean Hospital, and he has authored or co-authored more than forty peer-reviewed scientific articles.